GRANDAD

First published in November 2019

British Library Cataloguing in Publication Data
A catalogue record for this book is available
from the British Library.

ISBN 978 1 78521 233 8

Library of Congress catalog card no. 2019942918

Published by Haynes Publishing,
Sparkford, Yeovil, Somerset BA22 7JJ, UK
Tel: 01963 440635
Int. tel: +44 1963 440635
Website: www.haynes.com

Haynes North America Inc.
859 Lawrence Drive, Newbury Park,
California 91320, USA

Printed and bound in Malaysia

GRANDAD

ALL YOU NEED TO KNOW IN ONE CONCISE MANUAL

Andrew Parkinson

Contents

Chapter 1

A great role for the rest of your life

Grandads have a unique part to play in their grandchildren's lives, and the aim of this book is to help you play it with greater skill, confidence and enjoyment. What you do and who you are will mean that your role is both important and great fun, full of laughs as well as occasional tears. It can be very serious. And seriously silly.

Enjoy this gem of a role: polish up every facet and shine! And yes, everything here is fine for grandma, too. So if she's around, and maybe getting a wee bit jealous of what's in this book, let her in on it! There are scores of ideas and activities here for you all to enjoy and share for a long time into your grandchildren's lives.

Your new supporting role

When your first grandchild is born, you step into a new role. It has many names – Grandad, Grandpa, Da, Poot, Gumps, Gamps, Poppa, Wompa … the list is endless.

Whatever the name, it can be both a starring turn and a vital supporting role for a young family. Sometimes it'll be easy, sometimes slightly scary, sometimes quite serious, and always potentially full of interest, fun, laughter and – most important of all – love.

Your starring role may involve you making frequent appearances every week – to help out during the day or to babysit in the evenings – occasional days every month or two, or, if distance is a challenge, perhaps you make an important guest appearance only once or twice a year. Hands on, close by, from a distance … develop the role as best as you can, put in as much energy as you like, support the other family players and above all, be there for the little star from their very first appearance!

Why Grandad can be so important
VIP? Me? You've perhaps not thought of yourself as that. But once your first grandchild is born, you are likely to be one of the most significant people in your grandchild's life.

And it's also likely that you already have a lot of experience to bring to the party. You'll probably find memories of raising your own children flood back as the baby grows. In a way, this is a repeat performance of your own experience as a dad to young children.

You're in a unique position for a loving, caring focus. Develop it, and your grandchild may choose you above all strangers. You can be an adult they can rely on; you can really understand them; you can really know and love them, one of a highly select team backing the family.

Key supporter – but not the expert!
Remember, unless you work with children (and even if you do), you're not an expert on parenting your grandchildren. You may have great experience with your own

children, and that's very valuable, but it's mum and dad who will know most about your grandchildren, growing with them as you did with yours.

You may remember clearly some things from past experience. Be ready to adjust! Tactics to encourage good behaviour that worked with your children may not work or be appropriate with your grandchildren. Some will. Things that your children loved to do may not be a wow with your grandchildren. Some will.

We have selective memories. We tend to forget the bad times (unless they're really awful) and the failures (unless they were disastrous) in favour of happy, easy memories of happy, easy childhood times when things were always good. We forget what hard work it is being a parent, and how hard it is not to get enough sleep!

A sympathetic ear

This time round, you don't have the emotional turmoil – or sleep deprivation – of being a new parent. Do you remember the shock of carrying a baby out of hospital or off into the outside world for the first time, realising the tectonic plates of your world had now irrevocably shifted? Can you remember being hit by the scary truth that you were now definitely a grown-up? You've been there. And there'll be many feelings that the parents have that you can identify with. These equip you for the vital job of supporting the parents.

A first-time dad often feels out on a limb, at a loose end – where does he fit in now? Talking about it may help him enormously. Keep reassuring him how much he too matters to the baby.

You're a special role model. After dad, you may possibly be the only consistent male role model in your grandchildren's lives, depending on if, and how frequently, the other grandad and any uncles make their appearances. Teachers come and go, and before they start school, young children typically mostly experience females and other mums at playgroups and pre-school groups.

... and a memory keeper

One task and privilege is that you're helping to build a platform of family memories that your grandchild can stand on firmly for the rest of their lives. Your story will give them a clearer sense of identity and self-confidence. You have a valuable, unique collection of memories that your grandchild can tap into.

There are great opportunities for sharing your – and their – experiences. These may involve doing things or just talking how you felt about things, both of which will create common ground with your grandchildren. Tell them what scared you, how you were angry about things, and they'll tell you too. Let them into your life, so they'll let you into theirs.

Gifts to invest, with great returns

Time is a gift to invest. As adults, we usually want to do things quickly and efficiently. Parents love it if you're not in a hurry. The activities in this book will usually take you ages longer with little helpers than if you were to do them by yourself. But that's the point – it's the doing things together that makes it doubly rewarding for both of you.

Having plenty of time for grandchildren makes them and you feel extra special. It gives affirmation of your love to the child and creates great memories. Many teenagers say that one of the things they remember most fondly about their grandad was that he had – and maybe still has – lots of time for them.

Adding risk and excitement

Grandfathers and fathers have a distinctive part to play in fun and games. While mums and grandmas are typically quite gentle in their nurturing and averse to risk taking, men often engage in much more physical types of games – albeit (hopefully) in a safe and controlled manner.

Throwing children in the air, swinging them around, pretending to drop them – these high-octane games produce giggles and squeals of delight and allow babies and children to experience a wider range of feelings. What's more, activities like these actually trigger chemical changes in the brain that are excellent for a baby's development. Older children, too, really thrive on rough-and-tumble play, chasing and play fighting, and through the experiences learn the boundaries of their capabilities

An honorary grandad?

Whether your own grandchildren are near or far away, you can offer your time to other families, perhaps single-parent ones, or a family whose grandparents live far away. As an honorary grandad, you can enjoy the privilege and fun of sharing the lives of other young children as they grow up.

The other grandad

If the other grandad is around, that can be a huge plus for a child. Remember, you're not in competition. Whether you're in direct touch with him or you only hear things through the parents, it's good to identify where your different interests and skills can complement one another.

Supporting mum and dad

Remember, they're the parents...

The parents will set rules and routines and boundaries. You might not agree with the detail, but you need to follow and respect them. Support, don't compete. You're not trying to be a better parent than you were: help *them* be better parents – and they can help you be the best grandad.

Hear and obey. Be ready to take orders and be led (sometimes by the parents, later by the child). Be a great team player, not the boss.

Only give advice if it's clearly asked for. When you do, offer it in such a way that it can be taken or rejected in a way that everyone is happy about. Use phrases such as: 'do you think...', 'I wonder whether...', 'this might help...'. Don't be upset if they say 'no thanks'. Name jobs

Seal the deal

Think of putting a great SEAL on your relationship with the parents. Always:

S upport them
E ncourage them
A ccept and agree with them
L earn with and love them.

you can do, practical help or financial assitance might be appreciated but difficult to ask for. Offer to help, both generally and picking out specific jobs. Can you buy the cot or help decorate the house? And don't be irritated if the offer is turned down.

Make sure you keep on getting on

There are a few golden rules that should help maintain harmony during your visits:

- Don't outstay your welcome. Whether you stay for a long or a short visit, agree its duration beforehand, and don't be surprised if things change.
- Develop a thick skin and don't take offence.
- Be ready to say sorry. If you've caused any upset, and if you're not quite sure why, gently find out why later, once things have calmed down.
- Bite your tongue. There will be many occasions when you might think: 'I wouldn't do that'. Think it, don't say it.
- Don't take sides – either with mum or dad, or with child against parent.
- Encourage and praise the parents.

Online advice and real conversations

It can be annoying to find your advice discarded in favour of information found online. Some parents rely heavily on websites and take them as gospel; just because it's seen on screen can make material seem more believable or authoritative than it really is. However, the information is not always of a high quality. People sometimes recommend things on the basis of virtually no experience, sometimes because they want you to copy them, or they may have their own agenda. When it comes to general parenting advice, online information is rarely as good as a two-way conversation with real friends.

New mothers often feel quite isolated. Many, having just stepped out of work, do not have much of a support structure locally. Encourage her to find out about local community, church and other voluntary groups for mothers and babies. These provide a great opportunity for sharing experiences and seeing how other babies develop, and can lead to very valuable friendships as well as a lot of fun.

Tuning in to children

Babies are truly amazing. Their brains develop so fast: during the first six months they double in size, and by the age of three they will have grown to about 80 per cent of their full adult size. This is therefore a crucial time: a baby uses every experience to learn and increase brainpower. The first year is also key in terms of language development, even though they probably won't speak a word.

Fascinating and beautiful

If you're lucky to enough to be around, you can experience again the first weeks and months of a child's life. It's a rare privilege to be there, close up. Look into the baby's eyes: eye contact actually makes the brain grow – every time you lovingly hold their gaze! After a couple of weeks, they can focus on your face, about a foot away. As the weeks go by, continue to smile, laugh, croon and start making funny faces; they'll soon start imitating you.

A crying baby...

You may be surprised, but grandparents are often naturally really good at settling a crying baby. This fact can be very helpful for parents – but also quite demoralising.

When babies cry vigorously, their heart rate and blood pressure increase – and their cries trigger the same reaction in the mother, but not in other adults. This is a scientifically observed specific physical

and emotional response that ensures the mother responds to the cries. Always tell this to a new mum and remind her that it's because she is so well attuned to her baby that the crying really upsets her. Unfortunately, of course, her upset can sometimes play back to the baby in a kind of emotional short circuit that can see both crying longer, which is when it can be useful for someone else to step in and soothe the baby, if appropriate.

By contrast, you and grandma will probably be nowhere near as upset by a baby's cries: the baby senses this, and also senses from smell and sight that this isn't mum any more. Yet you can often provide what baby wants – touch, closeness, warmth, reassurance – and stepping in may well help everyone calm down sooner (unless of course the baby is hungry).

Before long, most mothers get used to the crying and are able to calm the baby and themselves more easily. However, if she's very short of sleep or otherwise stressed, it's likely that your help will still be very valuable – so long as the mother still feels that she is by far and away the best carer for her baby.

The crying debate

You might remember – it was once considered fine to leave a baby crying for long periods, until they finally went to sleep. Some people thought that you could 'spoil' the baby by giving them too much attention. The fact is, though, you can't spoil a baby under the age of one, and children under two in general cry not to be annoying, but because they need to be comforted or to have a need met.

Of course, this is an area of debate, however, so do listen to the parents as they may have chosen to do some form of

Cuddles and kisses

Some men are naturally reluctant to touch, cuddle and kiss babies and small children, and this is fine. What's more, if there's any hesitation about it from mum or dad, of course you must respect this – and not take it personally. However, many parents are happy for you to be quite physical in your play. Children love it, too, and you're in a great position to provide extra affection in their lives.

It's even good medicine: if you hug and kiss a small child after it has fallen over and grazed its knee, you release calming chemicals in the child's brain, which all combine to reduce pain and restore calm. It also makes a child happy and strengthens your bond with them.

sleep training – which can and does work in some situations, and may involve controlled crying. This is stressful enough as it is, and your views are likely to be unwelcome, however well-intentioned.

'Clingy' babies

For the first six months or so, most babies are usually quite happy to be passed from one adult to another. From about the age of eight months, however, they become more discerning, and 'clingy'. It's an important natural stage: babies aren't mean to be independent! For this reason, from the age of eight months to about two-and-a-half years a baby naturally becomes wary of strangers. Unless you are around a lot, they may treat you as a stranger. Don't worry: stay in their company, along with their parents, and they'll soon be comfortable with you again.

Baby talk – from birth!

Baby noises

The noises you make are sweet music for a baby. From about the age of three months onwards, your grandchild is absorbing all the sounds around them, and you can help them to grow mentally by talking to them – as much as you can. At first you may feel foolish and they may not have much idea of what you're talking about, but by the age of two they'll understand more and more and it will gradually become a two-way conversation.

If you're stuck for words, just talk to yourself out loud – it doesn't matter what about – or start making up stories. And don't feel stupid if you find yourself using a sing-song tone when talking to them: it's

sometimes called 'motherese' and studies show that babies respond best to this. They won't think you're mad.

Humming your love

From the first few days after birth, babies respond to singing and humming, and the deeper voice of a man can be particularly soothing and interesting.

As well as walking around, rocking a baby and singing or humming generally to him, there's a simple game you can play that combines sound with action. Baby can be lying or propped up. Keep your eyes on him. Hold both of his hands and move them up and down while changing the pitch of your humming with the movement. Any change is fine; you don't need to be in tune. Do the same, this time moving the baby's hands side to side. Repeat, but with the legs. Select the movements depending on the baby's age, temperament and mood – very gentle and soothing or quite energetic and bouncy.

Smiles – 'it's just wind'

It used to be that when a very new baby seemed to smile, a knowledgeable adult somewhere would spoil it and say: 'It's just wind'. Nowadays, experts confirm that's not true. Very small babies do smile – and your grandchild may be trying to smile at you within a couple of weeks!

Some babies communicate by little smiles when you smile at them when they are very tiny – only weeks old. This may not yet be a broad smile, but slight muscle movements. Remember, it isn't necessarily wind – though they also 'smile' then too. Make sure you smile and talk back.

Sharing secret blinks

Some babies will communicate through blinking from an early age. When your grandchild is about two months old, try synchronised blinking. If they blink, you blink back. If you blink a slow blink, they may do the same. It can work with older babies, too, before they can talk!

Fun with movement

Once they've learned to focus, probably by three months, small babies love following movement, especially if it ends up with a surprise. This is why games such as Round and Round the Garden are a success.

Background noise

If you're looking after a baby, having the television or radio playing in the background is thought by some to be bad for them, since it can be confusing and distracting. Quiet music at bedtime is different, however, and can provide a useful trigger for a child to get to sleep. There is a disadvantage, though: if the child is 'hooked' on some particular music, they can find it hard to get to sleep without it.

Now we are one

Wonderful words, words, words

The second year of a child's life is remarkable for language development. By 18 months, they'll probably have a vocabulary of about 200 spoken words, and understand thousands more. By two years, this will have doubled. They're picking up words daily, and will soon probably understand more than 1,000. By three, they're getting easier for adults outside the family to understand, and by four, most children speak fluently.

The more you talk to a child at an early age the larger their vocabulary will be by the time they begin school. It provides a great start. Take all opportunities to chat, even during the early months when the baby can't talk back. When they're sitting up and doing clever things, praise them not just with a 'well done' or 'good', but with extra words, for instance 'lovely clapping' or 'well done, what a tall tower'.

Childproof or child-friendly home

You can try to make your home childproof. When they're a baby, it's easy, but then they start crawling…. After that, as your grandchild grows up, essentially you have two choices: make more places out of bounds as their reach and strength increases, or make more places safe and child-friendly. The latter is often the better option. It's easier to put that precious vase up in the attic for a few years than to keep little fingers from admiring it too closely when nobody is looking.

You can lock or barricade some rooms. That could be safe. But there's always the possibility of forgetting to turn a key or block a door – and, oh bliss – inadvertently leaving open an Aladdin's cave for young visitors.

You can also adjust according to each child: this child may love pulling books off shelves for a few months, so you can remove them; that one may be drawn to pot plants – scattering soil is so very interesting; another one has a fascination for remote controls. And hiding them. So you need to hide them first.

Remember, making your home fairly child-friendly is kind to the parents – otherwise they can't really relax. From around the age of two, a sensible precaution is to realise that nothing below about 2m/6ft is safe. Some children are natural explorers and mountaineers, who learn to climb on chairs, and shift them around rooms. Things can move fast.

Eight months to two years

'Attachment' is used in child development terminology to describe what happens emotionally first between a mother and her baby, and later between the baby and other adults.

Think of it as the relationship that starts when a baby expresses a need by crying and the mother responds with affection and confidence, not to mention milk! If it all starts well, and the vital first relationship between mother and baby is comfortable and contented, then the baby experiences the world as a safe place. They understand that they can trust other people. They feel valued, treasured, worthwhile.

This is secure attachment, and is absolutely the best experience a baby can have. So, you may ask, how can you as a grandad be important for the development of your little ones? Up to around the age of three, a baby flourishes with full-time attention from loving close adults. Mum and dad can probably provide for most of the physical and emotional needs, but additional loving adults who will be there constantly in their lives can improve both the quality and quantity of care for a child.

The first three years of a baby's life are crucial for brain development and a positive, healthy childhood. Any loving

adult stimulation is extremely valuable. Intelligence and character depend on experiences and influences from significant people. Put simply: the more loving and positive stimulation a child enjoys, the more opportunities she or he will have to develop.

Grandparents – really great for childminding

Whether or not parents decide/need to go back to work is entirely their business, but what you can do, if possible, is offer your services to help out. Grandparents can be wonderful childminders, providing a close, loving, highly personal level of familial care – so long as you are physically and mentally up to the considerable challenge of course, and live close enough to be able to do it on a reliable, long-term basis.

A new arrival

When there's a new baby in the family, it's a great time for grandparents to shine with the older children! A once-single child finds gets quite a shock when they're no longer the centre of attention. It's like they've been knocked off a pedestal and they're not quite sure where they stand now.

They'll therefore hugely appreciate it if you give them more attention than you perhaps did before, play in a more concentrated way with them, and show more interest in them than the baby. Golden rule when you go to meet a newborn: bring a present for older children as well as the imposter, I mean baby.

Tears, tantrums and 'terrible twos'

People often call the third year of a child's life the terrible twos. This is a pity. It's a year when there is remarkable development in speech and movement – and personality. The problem is that the parents have to adapt and learn how to cope with a child who's testing boundaries, developing independence and finding out which actions produce results.

From about the age of two, children develop self-awareness. They become little independent people. And this means they want to get their own way. Or feel clumsy or helpless. So they get upset. Really upset.

A tantrum is a dramatic tactic for attention seeking. The best way to handle it is to withdraw attention. If it's a good option, you can walk a short distance away or put the child in another room. Don't cajole, lose your temper, shout, scold or threaten.

Tantrums don't usually last long. Wait for the storm to subside, and then talk. Find out why they felt upset, help them to put things into words, because it's often their inability to explain themselves that causes or adds to the outburst. It can be very helpful if you suggest things like 'I wonder if you were angry because …'

Technoference – are you switched on to children?

A mobile phone is a wonderful tool – if you are in control of it. But it can easily take over more and more of your time and focus. 'Technoference' is a term for interference caused by digital and mobile technology devices during time spent with another person. It's becoming a serious problem with parents and other adults in their interaction with children.

Recent studies show that mobile phones are causing parents to be less tuned in to their children, meaning that they are less able to spot signs of their children's changes in mood and behaviour. They are using less eye contact, which children need in abundance, and language skills are under-developed as children miss out on meaningful conversation with their parents.

Children typically react in two ways: they sometimes withdraw into themselves, or they start to play up, with challenging behaviours that are simply attention seeking. This often makes adults feel annoyed about being interrupted and drawn away from their focus of attention, their phone. The parent may continue to disregard the child, the child may play up more, and it can easily end up in anger and maybe tears.

Your actions speak volumes. Switch off your mobile while you're with a grandchild

and you're giving out a clear message. Switch your attention to your phone and you're switching off from the child. The time you have with your grandchild really is precious for both of you, so enjoy it, don't let yourself be distracted by a screen, which you can always turn to after their bedtime. And remember, if you don't want older children to switch away from you on their phones, you have to set a good example.

or 'Was something making you feel sad?'. Even when your guess is completely wrong, it will probably help the child towards verbalising their feelings. Which is half way to avoiding tantrums in the future.

Discuss, but don't argue about it. At this age, and probably in the mood they are in, there's little benefit pointing out that they're being unreasonable. These are very small beings, not rational adults! Acknowledge they are upset, perhaps be sympathetic – but be cautious about trying to make things better, because you don't want to reward the tantrum – it will only encourage more.

Family stories

Reading to – and with – children

It's a great privilege to follow a child's journey into literacy. Evening story time is particularly special. If you're lucky enough to be able to share the routine, enjoy it while it lasts!

You don't need to be great at reading out loud. Your focused attention is what is most precious to your grandchild. What's more, it's a lovely opportunity to sit side by side and enjoy a one-armed hug!

It's also fun to get a child to join in. From as young as two, you can encourage children to tell their own story from a picture book. They can 'read' from the pictures. Children can be very good at memorising stories: read out loud and have them join in and take over.

Tell me a story, Grandad!

Children love to be told improvised stories, so retell an old tale or improvise with a new one. Get children to suggest characters to get things rolling.

'READ BORING BOOK, GRANDAD'

Still awake? The following is a useful tactic at bedtime with a child who is slow to get to sleep. Get them to choose a book, read it in a dull monotone, and you may find it soothes them to sleep. Make sure you stay awake yourself though – it's easy to doze off!

SILLY READING

Children often ask for the same story again and again. You can spice it up by making silly mistakes accidently-on-purpose. Replace a word with another one and see if they realise; change the name of a character – they'll probably notice that; and pretend you made a mistake. It's a great game, fun for all participants. Just watch out, it's likely they'll tell on you... .

'Silly Grandad didn't read it properly, daddy!'

NOW THEY'VE STARTED TO READ

Make sure you listen to them reading. Your time will be invaluable here in helping your grandchild get along well at school – especially if their parents don't always have enough spare time or energy to invest.

'READ' THEM YOUR OWN STORY

Your grandchildren will become interested to know more about where they've

come from. Help chart their family history and heritage, at their pace. Use photos and documents to help tell the story. What were they like when they were babies? What were mum or dad like? What about uncles and aunts, and great-grandparents?

Writing to stay in touch

Make the most of phone calls and facetime to stay in touch – but not too often! It's like visiting: ensure you're welcome and don't stay too long or too often. And remember, children love receiving and reading letters, cards and postcards. They don't have to be long or newsy. You can include jokes and drawings. Just writing to them says: 'thinking of you with love'.

A photo wall for the family story

This can trigger some great conversations. Find somewhere to put up old photos – a door, wardrobe wall, fridge door. Don't make it permanent. Using Blu Tack, fix a variety of old and new photos on the display, and change it as time goes by.

You could also write captions, such as: 'Here's dad before you children were born'; 'Here's xxx just learning to walk'; 'Here's a cousin riding a pony'; 'Here's Grandad as a baby!'.

Prepare yourself, though, as this sort of exploration of the past may well provoke slightly tricky questions to answer, such as:

'Where was I before I was born, Grandad?'

Grandad's rules

Teenagers and adults often remember with great fondness that their grandparents were strict. Children are usually very comfortable with clear boundaries and rules, which can be part of rituals and routines for a family. They teach children to respect other people and different ways.

Be sensitive to the parents

If in any doubt, discuss the rules you'd like to set out with the parents, and always be ready to give way to the experts – mum and dad!

Be yourself

Establish your own boundaries, making sure they don't contradict or undermine their family rules, then stick to them. It's fine if you ask children to sit at the table when they're eating, say please and thank you, and have an unbreakable rule about TV in the mornings, but don't feel you have to take responsibility for 'good' behaviour. Be yourself, while also being consistent,

loving, considerate and caring, but firm with rules. Also, try to be accommodating, understanding and flexible – but not if it raises your blood pressure!

Food and drink

You'll probably be guided by their parents when it comes to what to give your grandchild to eat or drink. As time goes on, you'll probably want to offer different menus, but it's best to check with parents first. It's also a good idea to be aware of NHS guidelines on sugar and salt.

Some grandparents feel the need to feed children frequently with sweets/candy. If you do want to give them a treat, check with the parents first, rather than establishing a routine they are unhappy with. Also check first if, for instance, you want to take your grandchildren to a sweet or ice cream shop – it is, after all, something grandparents traditionally do! But don't make it too frequent: a treat ceases to be a treat if it becomes a habit.

And a habit is nowhere near as delightful as a treat.

Stay sensitive to parental wishes, and be cautious about indulging children in too much sugar. A small grab bag of sweets can contain as much sugar as the maximum daily recommended amount for a six-year-old. Look for other, non-edible, ways to treat children, such as an activity magazine or some stickers featuring their favourite subject (dinosaurs, unicorns, cars and the like).

'It's yucky, Grandad'

Children sometimes get into the habit of rejecting food, saying 'it's yucky'. This can be demoralising for parents. And it's rude. You could apply Grandad's rule: 'you're not allowed to say something is "yucky", but you can say "I'm sorry I don't like it", because that's fair and considerate'.

Learning to say no

The word 'no' is very important in your growing relationship with your grandchild. If you don't see a grandchild very often, you're more likely to want to say 'yes', and that's reasonable. However, if you don't say 'no' enough, you risk becoming a walkover! Children grow up learning to ask for more. They learn that pester power works. If you always give way to it, you set an undesirable precedent for you, and also their parents. It's a good idea to agree boundaries with the parents – what a child is or isn't allowed on a shopping trip, for example.

Screen time rules

Phone usage often causes problems with even quite young children. Pulling children away from their screens for a meal or other social activity – even a simple one-to-one conversation – can create tensions and explosions. It's therefore a very good idea to set strict limits for everyone (not just the kids – they'll reasonably challenge double standards!) on screen time in your home, preferably with mum and dad's agreement. And stick to them. After the initial shock, many teenagers admit they like it.

Some grandparents insist on mobiles being switched off and even locked away during a visit. There'll be grumbles, but if the precedent is set early enough, and it's a rule you follow yourself, it'll soon become the norm. Find what works for you, then stick to it.

Say 'Well done!'

Keep on the lookout for examples – small or large – of good behaviours, and praise children for them. Be specific where possible: 'I was really impressed that you helped your sister'; 'well done for tying your shoelaces by yourself'; 'thank you for listening to me and setting the table'. Everyone responds well to positive feedback, and it makes children in particular feel noticed and valued.

Staying on the right wavelength with your growing grandchild

Talking down to children

Some people talk to children in the same way as they would to adults. Some talk to them as though they are babies. Your own personal style with your grandchildren is one you have to establish yourself: there are no right or wrong ways of doing it. However, it's really good to listen to them carefully and to understand their ways of thinking and their perspectives. Try to get on their wavelength, and let them lead a conversation as often as you do. Ideally, you'll change your style of chatting as the years go on, to suit the child. And you'll enjoy increasingly grown-up conversations with children as they develop, which can be immensely rewarding.

Dominating the conversation

It's easy to slip into a conversation that isn't really a conversation at all: it's you telling them something. You probably have come across that with some adults. They tell you stuff. Then they tell you more stuff. And don't ask you things. It is frustrating. Try to ask open questions (see opposite), and avoid a whole series of statements that leave the listener passive, able only to nod or switch off. This becomes even more important if you want to stay on children's

Eye to eye: on a child's level

When interacting with children, try to maintain eye contact. And with small children, try kneeling down (that's if you know you'll get up again easily again!) while chatting, so you are on their level. Doing so makes you much more approachable from the child's point of view.

wavelength as they grow into adolescence. Allow silences – don't rush in!

Watch your language...

No, this isn't about not swearing in front of the children! It's about using vocabulary that is appropriate to their age and understanding. Watch out for words that cause children to switch off, because they are too grown up or confusing. Listen carefully to what children are saying, the words they use, and take the

Open and shut

Try to use 'open' questions. A closed question merely encourages a yes/no response and can shut down a conversation. An open question, by contrast, opens up a conversation. Open questions often start with the words 'who', 'why', 'what', 'when' or 'how', and encourage interesting answers.

Who likes sausages?

This is a fun, simple icebreaker for children aged two to five, which is especially useful if you haven't seen your grandchild for a while and they are being a bit shy. It's very simple and something a young child will really enjoy, which will bring you together on the same wavelength.

Ask: 'Hands up, who likes eating…' and name a food. Keep going with several things, then add a surprise, such as: 'Hands up who likes eating … stones?!' 'Don't you like stones?!' You're guaranteed a giggle.

Continue, and this time you can put up your hand for normal things, then 'accidently' put your hand up for something funny.

'Mummy, does Grandad really eat snakes? I thought not. Snakes eat people, not the other way around. Silly Grandad.'

lead from them. Remember things they have said and be ready to repeat their words and phrases.

Comfortable chats with children

As adults, we tend to talk to children, not chat with them. We often direct a conversation, not giving them enough time to make the running themselves.

It's worth having in your mind some age-appropriate questions that could lead to a good chat. Otherwise, it's easy to slip into closed questions about school, which are often boring for the child and a bit of a dead end!

You can build up a repertoire of questions that can lead into interesting conversations, for example:

'If you had a million pounds, how would you spend it?'

'If you could go anywhere in the world, where you go?'

'What's the latest thing on social media – will you show me?'

A magic phrase: 'I didn't know that'

Children often say things that aren't quite right, or even that are totally wrong. Your instinctive reaction? Probably to say it's not true. However, instead of contradicting them, just say: 'I didn't know that'. Doing so puts you on a pleasant equal footing with the child, and that's nice. Later, you could gently question an idea or fact, if you really need to, but by saying: 'I didn't know that' you've shown the child that you're thoughtful and don't know everything!

What's more, in many cases the child will have gleaned the misinformation by not quite understanding a teacher or another adult, so by saying: 'that's wrong' you not only undermine the child, but also the authority from whom they believe they got the information.

These kinds of questions can be great for getting on a child's wavelength, whether they are 3 or 13. Children are usually very pleased to share their interest with you. They're used to most adults having only having a superficial interest: show them you're different.

'Would you like to show me your room?'

If you haven't been in their home for a while, asking a child to see their room is a great way of getting up to date with them. They'll show you new things, you'll see toys they're playing with now and get a sharper picture of their lives from books and trinkets on shelves and things on the wall.

Children – even teenagers – usually love it that you show so much interest. It makes them feel special. And it can open up some great conversations.

'When I was a boy'

However fascinating you may think it is, telling stories from your childhood risks being rather boring to a child. Keep the detail for when a child actively asks about your childhood, or when they're studying a topic at school and you can throw in some personal experience that suddenly becomes interesting and relevant to what they're learning.

Managing challenges
POSITIVE REFUSALS

It's easy to feel that you are a grumpy old grandad who keeps saying 'no'! Here's a useful technique that often works, and lightens up the situation: turn a 'no' into a 'yes'! It's a bit of a cheat but if you do it regularly, you'll probably have more amenable children, and you'll quickly get the hang of it. How? Try responding positively in a similar manner to the list of examples below:

> 'Can we go the park?'
> 'Yes, this afternoon.'
> 'Can we have some sweets?'
> 'Yes, but not until after dinner.'
> 'Can we watch TV?'
> 'Yes, later, when you have cleared up.'

Promises, promises

We often promise things that are not completely in our control to deliver. And things go wrong. Result? Disappointment, upset, anger. Quite reasonable.

A very useful technique is to promise less, and then deliver more. Set a child up for something that is alright or a mild disappointment, then deliver something better. For example, if you tell a child that mummy will be home before bedtime, then if the traffic's bad and she is late you may end up with an anxious, upset child on your hands. Tell her that mummy will be home in the morning, though, and you'll have a delighted child if mummy arrives before bedtime.

Life often feels full of little disappointments to a child. So turning these into positive surprises is lovely. For example, if the weather is looking poor but might pick up, warn a child they may not be able to go to the park, and then delight them with the news that you can go after all once the weather is better.

'Time to stop now'

Imagine. You're watching a favourite TV programme, then someone suddenly comes in, switches the television off and says: 'Time to stop now'.

That's similar to a scenario that is acted out probably daily in every play park in the

---

'Grandad, I'm bored'

Learning to handle boredom is an important life skill. It's great to encourage 'stickability' in children! In fact, helping them to do so will improve their concentration and patience, both of which will be valuable at school and in later life.

DO YOU REALLY NEED TO 'HELP'?
When children grow tired of one activity, let them find something else without your help – and congratulate them for their good idea.

Finding something different for the child or joining in won't boost their self-reliance or develop independence, so don't come in and entertain with interesting diversions or stimulating activities. Let them learn to entertain themselves.

BOREDOM OR FRUSTRATION?
Often, a child gets stuck with something and wants to give up. A little nudging from you might help. Maybe you can show there's a satisfying goal if they stick with it – a clear benefit in not giving up now. And praise at the end. Just ensure the triumph of completing a task is theirs, not yours.

TIME TO STOP?
Congratulate them for playing so long alone if they've definitely had enough.

country. A child is happily playing. An adult says: 'Time to go now'. The child objects. There's a row. The two end up leaving with at least one of them angry or in tears.

Here's a useful method for keeping everyone happy. When you want to call an end to an activity, give a child advance notice. If you want to send them off in a good mood, think **SEND:**

S **Specify** e.g. 'We must go in ten minutes.'

E **Explain** e.g. 'We need to go to catch the bus.'

N **Negotiate** e.g. 'OK, just five more minutes.'

D **Decide** e.g. 'We need to go now.'

Doing things this way is considerate, caring and firm, and can easily help avoid misbehaviour and tears.

'Hurry up, we haven't got all day'

A huge advantage for many grandparents is that they have a lot of time for their grandchildren, often more than the parents. So, you may find that many activities parents find stressful can be easier for you. For example, if you have enough time, food shopping with small children can be a great pleasure, one in which they can help find things and discuss what to get, help fill a trolley, hand over the money and get the change, carry things in a pushchair, and so on. But it can take ages.

From the age of two-and-a-half upwards, you'll often find a willing helper in all kinds of tasks: some that you might consider boring can be really interesting to a child. Wherever you can, let children help. It's a great investment for the future. It just takes time. It's easy to focus on going from A to B and forget that the journey can be as interesting as the destination.

Get on the child's wavelength and don't hurry them – unless you really haven't got time! Allow a two-year-old to make amazingly slow progress on a walk. Stroll through town, and there may be lovely diggers to watch. You haven't got all day, but there's no need to hurry.

Sharing passions

Many teenagers say that among their fondest memories of their grandads was them sharing their particular interests. So, it's valuable to share your passions with your grandchildren, and to introduce them to your special interests.

That said, it's easy to become a bore. Adjust what you share to the age and interest of the child. Make the story a simple one. Go into detail only if the child asks. Know when to stop.

Set the level to that of the child. Are you an angler? Your grandchild may enjoy learning about knots. You might choose a fishing trip that's most likely to produce results, such as mackerel fishing off the coast. Long waits and small children rarely go happily together! Keen on football? Many children like both watching and playing football, so do both. If they enjoy accumulating loads of information to show off to other people, read factual books with them or take them to a museum/gallery/source of more information.

Whatever subject you love, you can probably make it more interesting by focusing on some superlatives: what's the biggest, the fastest, the oldest, most valuable and so on – these catch the imagination.

'Grandpa used to tell us about all kinds of things, especially fossils. It was pretty boring but we didn't mind.'

Staying in tune – despite unsocial media

As children get older, they naturally tend to pull away from adults, giving their attention to their peers. What's more, they'll typically become more absorbed in social media and/or computer games, all of which can make them very unsociable.

What can grandad do to try to avoid losing touch with them? It may feel that they're in a very alien world. So, ask if they'll introduce it to you. Something that they are very into can become something that you show some interest in. If they'll allow you to, spend concentrated time with them. Encourage them to explain the latest trends, a new platform, an exciting piece of kit.

It's also a nice example of tables turned: you used to be the one who knew a lot, now it's the younger ones who are experts in their special subjects. It can be enjoyable for all, and they'll appreciate your interest – and admiration. They'll relish displaying their superior knowledge. In return, you'll learn a lot, with regular updates on a fast-moving world, and on a family level, you'll be more likely to stay in tune, even with teenagers.

'What's this for, Grandad?'

Grandad's treasures

You can set up a special drawer or box of fascinating things for the kids to fiddle around with. From about the age of four to well into their teens, kids love rummaging around. Choose objects that are interesting; they may trigger interesting conversations. Examples could include magnets, old watches, penknives, fountain pens, old coins, compasses, old drawing instruments, a gemstone collection, stamps, even buttons – whatever you have a collection of and that is safe for them to handle.

Praise and encouragement for children – and parents too

'I think that's a lovely picture of Grandma.'

For the first three years or so, your grandchild will thrive on loving praise. After that, they'll start to benefit hugely from a mixture of praise and encouragement.

What's the difference? Parents and grandparents consistently praise their children for doing things (not necessarily doing things well, just doing things). That's fine, but receiving praise means you're dependent on someone else: that person tells you how well you're doing. Your self-confidence hangs heavily on what they say. Unfortunately, children often receive praise for doing something that's not very good. For example, it's not great for a five-year-old to be praised for dashing off a scribbled drawing without care and attention.

By contrast, encouragement builds up self-confidence. It can come from positive statements that are not like judgements from on high. For example, rather than saying: 'that's beautiful writing', you could say: 'I think that's beautiful writing, it's so neat.'

The following are helpful tips to enable you to provide positive encouragement:

■ **'I' sentences** These really help in cases where it shows that something is

your opinion, not a judgement; a statement open to discussion, not an absolute fact.

- **Be specific** Encouragement can zoom in on things. Focus on something specific, say how much you like it.
- **Make comparisons and encourage self-criticism** For example: 'I think that drawing is even better than the one you did yesterday – what do you think?'
- **Build a picture** To a young footballer: 'That was a good tackle' is reasonable praise, but why not build it up: 'I thought that was a good tackle because you surprised the striker at the right moment'. This tells a child that a) their timing is good, and b) they're good at tackling.
- **Encourage the parents** Remember, too, that mum and dad will flourish with encouragement. Tell them things like: 'I

thought that was a very good way of handling that situation'. It may seem patronising, but if it's said in the right way, it will bolster their confidence in their parenting skills.

- **Loving motivation** Keep your eyes open to see where a child's doing well. Minor and major things – be sure to encourage them. And especially when things don't quite go right, encourage them. Show your faith in them. Don't give them a 'when I was a boy' story of heroic endurance, of failure finally leading to success. Keep that for Hollywood. In real life, it's probably not helpful. Just sympathise and encourage! Failure and disappointment are part of the real world. Don't ever say: 'I promise it'll be alright'. Instead, always assure them that you're on their side, that you'll love them, whatever!

Chapter 2

Great things to make and do indoors

Your home can be a treasure trove of great things to make and do. Make sure you transfer them to your grandchildren's homes, too, and carry on an age-old tradition – of grandads (imagined in books and movies, or in real life) who play games, do tricks and make lots of things!

Remember, it's the doing and having fun that's of prime importance! There are no prizes for perfection in projects with children. The main aim is for them to build up skills and abilities, which will help equip them physically and emotionally for all sorts of challenges at home, school, and even adult life.

Card games and tricks

With a pack of cards, you can keep children busy and happy, whether they're 3 or 13.

Catch the Crowns

A very simple game for 2–4 players (probably aged 5+), plus dealer. A very small child (3+) will enjoy being the only player.

You need a standard pack of cards. The players sit opposite the dealer, who shuffles the pack and gets ready to lay three cards on the table quickly, face up.

The players have to react fast: they are looking out for 'crown' cards: Jack, Queen or King. When they see one, they have to slap their hand down on that card before anyone else claims it. If they're first – maybe their hand is at the bottom of a pile of hands – they take the card and any in that pile. However, if they slap an incorrect card, they forfeit three cards, which go back to the dealer.

The dealer keeps on laying down cards in thee piles, and players build up their takings until all the cards are used up.

Memory Game

This game involves 1–3 players, from about age 3, using a standard pack of cards.

This is an old favourite. What makes it interesting is that you'll see your grandchild's thinking develop as time goes on. Their tactics will change from the age of about 3 to about 6, by which time they may have become quite skilled.

Spread out all the cards face down on a table. The aim is to remember where cards are and match them. Player one turns two cards up, says out loud (if they're old enough) what they are, then turns them back. Player two does the same, and so on, until someone spots a possible match. They turn both cards up and if they're a match, take them. That player has the next go.

Adjust this to the age and ability of your grandchild. Decide what constitutes a match. It could be the same number or rank, from different suits. It could be same number or rank from the same colour. It could be all court cards. To make it very easy for smaller players, it could be all cards from the same suit, or even all cards with the same colour.

Beggar My Neighbour

Also charmingly called Strip Jack Naked, this is good for all ages from about 5+. It involves two players, using a standard pack of cards.

This game requires no skill, just fun. The aim is to collect as many cards as possible and see your opponent run out of cards. Children love its simplicity. You need to remember to appear to get upset about losing all your precious cards, as that adds to the fun!

Divide the pack of cards roughly in half. Each player has their cards on a table, or holds them, face down. Players take turns to turn over their top card and play it face up in the centre of the table, building up a pile.

There are two kinds of card: 'pay' cards and 'ordinary' cards. Aces, Kings, Queens and Jacks are pay cards. All the rest are ordinary cards.

Play continues until someone turns over a pay card. The other player has to pay for this card by giving cards to their opponent, as follows:

4 ordinary cards for an Ace
3 ordinary cards for a King
2 ordinary cards for a Queen
1 ordinary card for a Jack.

When that player has paid up, the first player takes the whole pile and puts it face down underneath his own cards.

If, while paying for a card, a player turns over another pay card, the previous pay card is cancelled, and his opponent has to pay for the new pay card instead.

The winner is the player who ends up with all the cards – or with the most cards if the game, which can go on for ages, has a time limit.

Learning to lose

We're all encouraged to be good losers, right? But the truth is, losing isn't much fun, whatever your age. And it's very hard when you're a child.

Card games are a great way of teaching children to lose with good grace. The best way of doing this is by making sure that a child wins enough times – sometimes by a bit of subtle manipulation to your disadvantage! The ideal win/lose ratio varies with each child, but a child under eight will probably thrive on winning three games out of four, while one aged 10 will be happy winning just two games out of four. Help them to become content to win less and lose more by congratulating them on their play.

Cheat

Good for all ages from about 8+. Use a standard pack of 52 cards without jokers for 2–4 players. If there are more than 4 players, shuffle two packs together.

Deal out all the cards. Some players may end up with one or two more cards than others: that's fine. The aim of Cheat is to get rid of all the cards in your hand.

Allow time for each player to look at their cards and sort them in order. The first player starts a discard pile: they discard one or more cards, put them face down on the pile, and say what they are – 'two Aces, one King' etc. But they may be lying.

The first player must discard Aces (or must say that's what he's doing), the second player discards Twos, the next player Threes, and so on. After Tens come Jacks, then Queens, then Kings, then back to Aces, etc.

As you discard cards face down, you don't necessarily use the cards you claim you're putting down. For example, if you need to discard a Ten and don't have one, you can actually discard any card or mixture of cards.

But beware of being rumbled. Anyone who suspects that what's being discarded isn't what it's claimed to be can challenge the player by saying 'Cheat!'. The challenged player then has to reveal the card(s) they've just discarded. If they *are* what they were claimed to be, the challenge is wrong, and the challenger has to pick up the whole discard pile; but if any of the played cards are different from what was claimed, then the player whose cheat has been exposed has to pick up the whole discard pile.

After an incorrect challenge, play continues with the next player putting down any cards he chooses. The first player to get rid of all his cards and survive any challenges wins. Consequently, the last cards can be your downfall. If someone challenges you when you play them and you turn out to be a Cheat, then you have to pick up the whole pile and play continues.

Automatic magic:
The 21-card Trick

This is more maths than magic, but the effect is excellent. You can do it after minimal practice, and can easily teach it to children. What happens: you hold some cards in a pack, someone picks one, then they put it back anywhere. Within a couple of minutes, you magically find it again.

Start with a pack of any 21 cards. Ask someone to pick a card, let them show it to everyone else, and then return it anywhere in the pack. Tell them you're going to deal out the cards face up, and ask them to look out for their card as you do so but not to say anything if they see it.

1 Deal the cards face up in three piles, dealing from right to left. Then ask which pile the card was in. Take that pile, and put it between the other two as you pick up all three piles.
2 Repeat Step 1.
3 Repeat Step 1.

4 Pick up the three piles and again put in the middle the pile that you're told the card is in. Holding all of them, turn the whole pack face down and count (in your head) ten cards. Then say something that sounds appropriately magicky, like: 'I feel some tingling here', and with a flourish show the 11th card, which should be the one that was originally picked out.

How does it work? It's quite simple: all the shuffling just puts the card exactly in the middle of the 21-card pack – i.e. it becomes the 11th card.

Lost and Found

This is another very simple trick, which with minimal practice bamboozles children and adults alike. You destroy a card and magically make it reappear.

You need two identical cards from two packs and a table. When no one is looking, well in advance, hide one of the cards somewhere in the room in an envelope.

Hold up a pack and pretend to pick a card randomly, but simply take it from the bottom, having put the duplicate there.

Explain that you are going to practice some magic. Make up a performance. Ask someone to get a pair of scissors. Have a child or two help you cut up the card, pretend you're worried, then throw the

pieces up in the air and say 'Hey presto' and look surprised when nothing happens.

Do it again two or three times, then point somewhere and say 'over there'. While everyone is looking, slip the pieces into one hand, and into your pockets, pretending to hold them in the other hand. Now pretend to throw them in the air, and look surprised when they have all gone. Say that you're very sorry, we'll never see the card again and your magic didn't work. And then – 'Wait a minute, I can hear something ... can you hear something – I think it's coming from over there', and direct a helper to find your hidden card.

Amazing, your magic worked, you've put the card together!

Magic Paper Rings

You can teach children from the age of about six to do these tricks with paper rings. Anyone will find them intriguing: the results are surprising.

You will need
- white or coloured paper
- scissors
- adhesive tape
- pencil
- ruler

1 Make three strips of white or coloured paper about 120cm/48in long and 5cm/2in wide. You can do this for each strip by simply cutting up an A4/Letter sheet lengthways in four (fold in four or mark with a pencil) and taping the pieces together.

2 Draw a line all along the middle on one side of each of the three strips.

3 Tape the two ends of each strip together, so as to make three different types of ring: one has no twist; one needs a single twist; one a double twist. Make a small mark on each to distinguish which is which.

Ring number 1 – with no twist. Ask a member of the audience to help cut it.

Ring number 2 – with one twist. Explain to the audience that you'll cut the ring in two. Ask them to guess what the result will be. Cut slowly – you can invent a story as you do so. The result? You get one larger ring.

Ring number 3 – the ring with two twists. With someone's help, cut it as before. This time you end up with two interlinked rings. What a surprise!

The One-sided Piece of Paper

You will need
- white or coloured paper
- scissors
- adhesive tape
- coloured marker pens

Here's a delightful mathematical puzzle for everyone. How many sides does a strip of paper have? We all know the answer is two, don't we?

1 Make a smaller ring of paper: about 60cm/24in long and 4cm/1½in wide. Tape it with one twist in it.

2 Now, if someone draws a line on one side as far as they can, it will end up back at the beginning without a break! Try it again with a different coloured marker. It's a puzzle known as the Mobius Strip – a piece of paper with only one side.

Chess Lite! Queen's Attack

Chess is a great game because it helps children learn to think ahead. However, it takes quite a long time for a child to get their head around the full game, so here's a great way to start. It's a battle between eight pawns and one Queen. Who'll be stronger? Your play will decide…

SETTING UP THE BOARD

Turn the board so that both players have a white square in their right-hand corner. Decide who will play the pawns and who will be the Queen.

HOW DO THE PIECES MOVE?

The Queen can move any number of squares in a straight line – forwards, backwards, sideways, or diagonally – to make a capture. Pawns can normally only move forwards one square at a time, except on the first move, when they can move one or two squares. To capture, they have to move one square diagonally, left or right.

THE AIM OF THE GAME

If you're the Queen, you've got to capture all the pawns before any of them reach your first row. If you're the pawns, you've got to get just one of them to reach the back row. Do so, and you've won.

STARTING PLAY

Set up a row of white pawns in their normal starting position, i.e. second row. Place the black Queen on her square on the other side. Pawns play first. They have to protect one another, since alone they are vulnerable. The Queen has to go into attack, as she's outnumbered. Take it in turns playing Queen or pawns. Play for the best of five games.

'Let's pretend...'

That's a call to action that every grandad will hear, and must obey!

Substitution

The great thing with children is that their imaginations are often much greater than an adult's. So let's pretend… Anything can be anything else. So you have a pretend tea party. Those DVD cases, they can be plates. Those pencils can be knives. Yellow Lego bricks, let's say they are bananas. Encourage their ideas and add a few of your own to generate more of theirs.

Mummies and daddies, doctors and nurses

Role playing imaginative games is hugely important to young children, and you can play many roles in their stories. It's helpful to them if you stay in the story and treat it fairly seriously, until you know they'd like you to get silly. You being a baby is sheer delight to a child.

Who's the boss?

Children love imaginative play where the adult is bossed around. Enjoy the role, let them tell you off, let them put you in prison, put you on the naughty step and make you (pretend!) cry…

Dressing up

Because most children have such great imaginations, props and clothes for dressing up in don't have to be at all accurate. Don't be held back just because there are wonderful costumes in toy

shops. Things that you make can be used for all kinds of role play. A Superman cape from a shop is only a Superman cape. A cape you make from a plain old pillowcase can be not just for Superman, but also Robin Hood, a king or a queen, great wizards and many more heroes.

Making dens

Remember, all you need are some sheets or blankets draped over a table, and you've created an instant fun space for play. Children love to make dens. Add sleeping bags or duvets, cushions or pillows. Here's a tent in the desert, a secret cave, a kitchen or a castle.

Where can I get all this stuff?

All the materials used in this and other sections are fairly easily obtainable from craft and model-making suppliers, from pound/bargain shops, and online. Some of the materials can be found in hardware and building supplies stores. Most of it is inexpensive.

Two very silly games

The Pooty Game

- Suitable for children aged 4–10
- 2–6 children plus 1 adult

This is a very silly, simple game that is usually a huge success. It's named after a dearly loved grandad. You need a fairly clear room and ideally a door to it. One person starts as Pooty – usually the adult. Pooty declares something he doesn't want the others to do, goes out of the room, and comes back in, and chases people round the room, who are – of course – doing it.

For example: 'I don't want anyone to jump up and down.'

Pooty leaves the room, everyone jumps up and down. Pooty walks in, is amazed to find what they are doing, pretends to be very cross and chases them round the room.

There are so many things that Pooty can tell you he doesn't want you do to do. For example: 'Nobody put cushions on their head'; 'No dancing like a ballerina'; 'I don't want anybody to lie still on the ground' and so on … and on … and on … until someone else takes over as Pooty or everyone's tired out.

The Going to Sleep Game

- Enjoyed by children as young as 2½ and up to about the age of 10
- This game can be played by 1 adult with 1–4 children

This is a close cousin to the Pooty Game, and is just as silly. Grandad sits in a chair or lies on a sofa. You pretend to be asleep. Snore a few times. You say 'Nothing is going to wake me up except…' and pause … then name an animal. (In preparation, you can try telling them that it can be even more fun if they try other noises first, but they probably won't listen.)

Within seconds, one or other child will start making that noise, whereupon you wake up and leap up to try to catch the culprit.

(If you aren't able to leap up, simply act cross and stretch out your arms to try to catch the children, who will automatically move closer.)

Pretending to be cross at being woken, you drop back into the chair or sofa and declare that you're going to sleep again and 'nothing will wake me up except' … pause … think … choose … will it be a very quiet mouse, will it be a sports car … or 'a dog!'.

You can do this again and again: one of the children may take over but usually they'll prefer you to stay in the leading role. The game can continue as long as you have new ideas or recycle old ones without people getting bored.

High-speed hats

Kids love dressing up: just one simple thing can transform make-believe play. You can create all sorts of classy headgear very quickly with few materials.

Pirate's tombstone hat

You will need
- thin A3 black card/stock (or, as shown here, white card painted black on one side)
- ruler
- pencil
- bowl or saucer about 30cm/8in in diameter, or a pair of compasses
- scissors or craft/utility knife
- ballpoint pen
- glue stick
- white paper
- masking tape

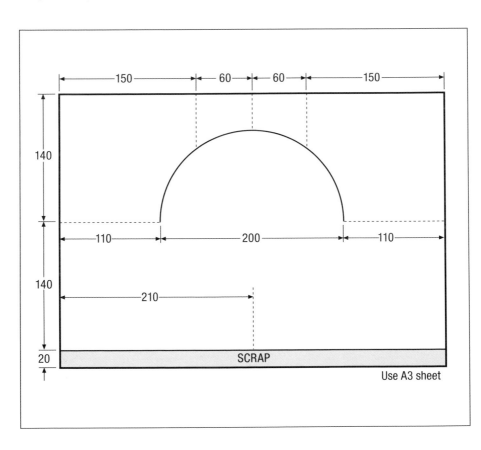

Use A3 sheet

1 Draw a line 15cm/6in from the bottom of the piece of card. Using a bowl or saucer, or a pair of compasses, mark a semicircle halfway along the line.

2 Cut around the semicircle with scissors or a craft knife. Score the line to either side, using the edge of the scissors or by pressing hard with a ballpoint pen.

3 Turn the sheet over and fold along the scored line, with the semicircle sticking up.

4 Decorate the hat using by glueing on shapes cut out of white paper, such as skulls, swords, crossbones, etc.

5 Fix three pieces of tape either side of

the long strip, to form a loop. You may also require tape at the bottom if you need to tighten the hat for a smaller head.

Quick crowns for princes and princesses

Every prince or princess needs a crown, and these simple coronets are sure to meet with royal approval.

You will need

- pencil
- ruler
- A4/Letter sheet of paper, dark colour or goldcraft/utility knife or scissors
- adhesive tape
- A4/Letter sheet of white paper ballpoint pen
- small piece of card/stock

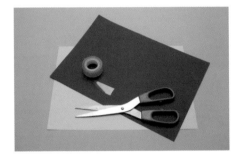

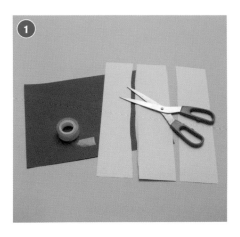

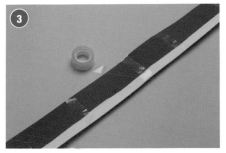

1 Measure and then cut two strips of coloured paper measuring 7.5 x 30cm/ 3 x 12in. Tape the two pieces end to end to make a very long rectangle.

2 Do the same with the white paper. Fold this strip lengthways in half and half again to create a band a little less than 2cm/¾in wide. It may help to score lines along the length with a ballpoint pen.

3 Fold the band in half so it forms a very long V shape. Insert the coloured strip into the V, and fix with tape.

4 Cut a row of triangles along the coloured paper from the top to the band.

5 Persuade the crown to curve into a circle by pulling the fold between thumb and finger several times, and make a ring.

6 Push the ends together to make the band the right size for your grandchild's head, then tape in position. Now it's their turn to make one for you!

'Which superhero would you like to be, Grandpa?'

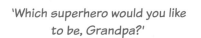

A circlet for a princess

Similar to the crown, this circlet is simple enough for children aged about 5+ to make by themselves, with supervision.

You will need

- three sheets of A4/Letter paper, in contrasting colours
- glue stick or adhesive tape
- pencil
- ruler

'Gramps says I'm clever because I do ballet and he can't. I don't think he's allowed.'

1 Fold and then cut one sheet of paper in half lengthways. Fold each half sheet into thirds along the length and tape them together.

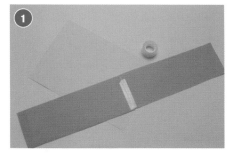

2 From one of the other coloured sheets, cut three strips about 1cm/½in wide along the length, then tape them together to produce a very long strip (about 90 x 1cm/36 x ½in).

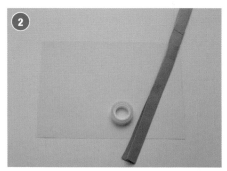

3 Wrap this strip around the band at a diagonal, then fix it with glue or tape at about 15cm/6in intervals and at the end. Trim the end.

4 Run the band between your thumb and forefinger to help it to bend. Bend it into a circle. Adjust the band to fit the child's head.

5 Draw and then cut out a diamond shape from the final piece of paper, then tape it to the front of the circlet so that it hangs down.

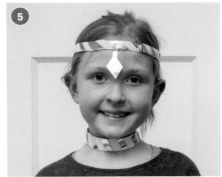

VARIATION: CHOKER AND BRACELET/ARMBAND

These follow the method used for the circlet.

- For the choker, make a circlet, measure it around the child's neck, then cut it so that it is about 4cm/2in longer. Make a 1cm/½in cut on the top of one end, and on the bottom of the other, so the two ends can slot together.
- For a bracelet or armband, you'll need a band measuring about 2.5 x 30cm/1 x 12in and a covering strip about 1 x 60cm/⅜ x 24in.

Capes and cloaks for heroes

Cloaks and capes are so versatile for dressing up, instantly transforming your little person into a superhero or lord!

You will need

- old sheet for a cloak, or an old pillowcase or towel for a cape
- marker pen
- pencil
- pieces of fabric, ribbon or duct tape for decorating (optional)

1 If using a pillowcase, cut it open along one long side and the bottom edge, to make a double-width sheet of fabric.

2 For a long cloak, measure the length

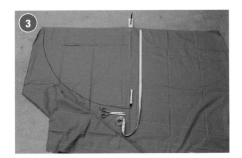

A bandana for a bandit

Don't forget, you can always turn a child into a swashbuckling villain in moments. Just make a bandana from a lightweight scarf or a strip of cloth about 60cm/24in long and tie it round your hero's head.

from shoulder to ankle. For a cape, take a measurement from shoulder to knee.

3 Use the measurement to draw a semi-circle on one edge of your sheet. To do this, cut string to about 5cm/2in longer than the measurement. Tie your marker to one end, and a loop at the other. Get an assistant to hold the string tied at one end to a pencil: draw your semicircle on the cloth holding the string taut.

4 Cut out the semicircle. Cut a slit in the sheet as shown in the photo, about 25cm/10in wide, just large enough to slip over the head.

5 Decorate by sticking or stitching on pieces of fabric or ribbon or duct tape.

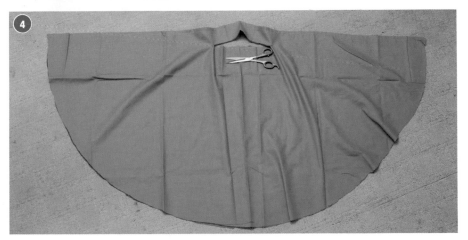

Games for a rainy day

Stuck indoors? Here's some fun to bring a little ray of sunshine into a rainy day, or whatever the weather.

What's in the Sack?!
- Suitable for children aged 4+
- 1–4 players

You will need
- pillowcase
- various objects (easily recognisable items, such as a fork and spoon, or weird things, such as cold pasta or a shelled hard-boiled egg)
- pens and paper

1 Out of sight of the contestants, put up to a dozen objects – more for older ones, fewer for younger ones – in the pillowcase.
2 The first contestant puts two hands in to feel the items (they mustn't look), and has 30 seconds to work out what they are.
3 They then write these down (or someone acts as scribe for younger children), and the next contestant has a go. Older children have just a minute to write their list. The winner is the child with the most complete list.

Kim's Game
- Suitable for children aged 3+
- 1 or more players

You will need
- up to 20 assorted objects
- tea tray
- pens
- paper

1 Place assorted objects on a tea tray, about 10 for younger children, up to 20 for older players.
2 Allow the player/s about 30 seconds to study the collection, then get them to leave the room.
3 Now remove several items. Call everyone back. Can they remember what's missing? Get them to tell you, or older ones can write a list. The winner is the one who remembered the most.

Hunt the Teaspoon/Hot and Cold

- Suitable for children aged 3+
- 1 or more players

Thimbles are not so common these days, so here's a simple alternative to a traditional game.

You will need
- teaspoon

1 Get someone to hide a teaspoon in an unlikely place in a room. The player/s then have to hunt for it, one at a time or in pairs. Since many children are delightfully unobservant, you may choose to provide help by saying 'hotter' or 'colder' the nearer or farther they get.
2 When they've found the spoon, it can be their turn to hide it or do it again.

Drawing on the ceiling

This is a lovely activity, especially at bedtime or when lounging about in bed in the morning. You need to draw, but you don't need pencil or paper!

1 Everyone lies flat, eyes up to the ceiling. You have to be all snuggled up together.
2 One person uses a pointed finger to draw a shape or letter in the air on the ceiling. The others have to guess what it is. You could choose a simple thing like a letter M or something complicated, such as a car. You could draw an outline – or some children go into extraordinary invisible detail.
3 Once you've guessed what it is, everyone takes turns, however they like.

Quizzes

Children love quizzes, as long as they know most of the answers. So, the challenge for you is to come up with interesting questions they can answer, suitable for their ages. If they are floundering, think of funny or simple clues.

It's also fun for them to be quizmasters and ask you fiendishly difficulty questions.

Roll a Robot

- Suitable for children aged 4+
- 2 or more players

The game of Beetle has been around for generations. Here's a new-generation, hi-tech version. Well, sort of.

You will need

- pencil or pens
- paper
- dice

1 The back story is that you are all managers of a robot factory. You have to build one as quickly as possible, but you need the components and can only get them by rolling dice.

2 The youngest player rolls both the dice first, then the other children follow in age order. The top scorer starts the game.

3 To start building your robot, you need a body first: from either dice, you have to throw a 1 or wait until your next go, and keep going until you get a 1.

4 Now you play, rolling just one dice, going round clockwise, aiming to draw a robot quickest. Numbers give you other components:

roll a 2 to draw an arm
roll a 3 to draw a leg
roll a 4 to draw the head
roll a 5 to draw an eye
roll a 6 to draw the mouth
(5 and 6 are only any good if you've already drawn the head)

5 As soon as you've completed your robot, call: 'I am a robot' in a robotty sort of voice. You've won that round. (You might want to continue your drawing with hands and feet and other robot parts and colour it in.)

VARIATION: ROBOT ASSEMBLY LINE

Suitable for children aged 7+; 2 or more players.

This is the same as Robot, but for older children, since you play with two dice. The aim is to build a set of three robots at the same time. If you're good at sums, you can add the numbers on the dice together to make numbers you want. For example a 3 and a 2 can make an arm and a leg, or an eye (5). The winner is the first to compete the assembly line of three robots.

As well as playing against others, this can be fun as a solo pastime.

Art and craft activities for every age

Home-made play dough

Play dough is very easy to make, and can provide hours of play (with not too much mess) for children aged about 2+.

You will need

- about 100g/8 tbsp flour
- 25g/2 tbsp table salt
- about 60ml/4 tbsp warm water
- 15ml/1 tbsp sunflower oil
- 15ml/1 tbsp cream of tartar (optional)
- a few drops of food colouring (optional)
- You will also need:
- mixing bowl
- spoon
- work surface
- plastic tablecloth
- various implements (see below)
- plastic bag or clear film/plastic wrap

1 Mix all the ingredients together in the mixing bowl to form a ball.

2 Transfer the dough to a work surface and knead it for 2–3 minutes, adding a little extra water if it's too firm, or flour if it's too sticky.

3 If you want to use the same food colouring for the whole batch, add it at the start. For different colours, divide the dough, then work it into the dough portions as you knead them.

4 For happy play, cover a table with a plastic tablecloth, and provide various implements, such as a rolling pin or thick dowel; children's cutlery; pastry cutters; toy building blocks; and any other objects good for pressing interesting shapes on to the dough.

5 After use, wrap the play dough tightly in a plastic bag or clear film and keep it in a cool place. It usually lasts for weeks.

Baking play dough

This recipe for play dough that you can bake is even more exciting than regular play dough for children aged 4+. It makes a small amount – perfect for collections of all kinds of little shapes. The bonus is that you can eat your creations, or you can paint them (but then don't eat them!) using waterproof acrylic paints.

You will need
- 60g/8 tbsp plain flour
- 2 tbsp sunflower oil
- 4 tbsp water (you may not need all of it)
- 4 pinches of salt

You will also need
- mixing bowl
- spoon
- rolling pin
- cutters (optional)
- baking tray
- plastic bag or clear film/plastic wrap

1 Preheat the oven to 140°C/275°F/Gas 1. Place the flour and salt in a bowl and add the oil. Add the water gradually until you get a firm dough.

2 Transfer the dough to a floured work surface and knead it for a couple of minutes, adding a little extra water if it's too firm or extra flour if it's too sticky.

3 Roll out the dough very thinly, then cut out shapes, or model small pieces with your hands.

4 Put your creations on a baking tray and bake for 15 minutes, or until they're beginning to brown.

5 Remove from the oven and leave to cool.

6 If you have any dough left over, wrap it in a plastic bag or clear film, then either give it to a friend or keep it for another time. The dough will keep for about a week.

What can we make?

Have a go at:
- baguettes, loaves and pies
- sausages and burgers
- apples, pears and bananas
- carrots and peas

Messy play

Playing with paints

It's often not possible in young children's homes, but if you have somewhere where messing around with paints is OK, go for it!

Paint blocks and liquid poster paints from bargain stores are a very good investment. Use glass jar lids, food packaging or proper palettes. Some (very good) paints are acrylic, but be sure to wash brushes and children's clothes well, as it become waterproof soon after drying.

If you don't have lots of newspaper, get a large plastic tablecloth – another very good investment. Have plenty of glass jars of water; make sure they are bottom heavy to minimise the likelihood of spillages.

Find things to spread the paint, such as brushes, sponges, cloths, spatulas – fingers and hands are good too. Expect the unexpected!

Playing with water

Water provides endless fascination for babies as soon as they can sit up, and children love playing with it for years.

Collect lots of plastic containers, funnels, measuring jugs/cups and the like. Encourage play in the bath, in the kitchen or in the garden. Older children will probably enjoy using food colouring to make magic potions.

Paper fun

Papier mâché can provide hours of fun and great results.
These two simple projects are an easy introduction. If they do stick at it
(and sometimes they will, literally) children can do more ambitious projects: you can find
plenty in craft books and on the internet.

Other paper projects require just a little folding, sticking and ingenuity.

Papier mâché Loch Ness Monster

This is very easy and quick, well suited for very young children, aged 2½+.

You will need
- scrap paper or newspaper
- bucket or large mixing bowl
- PVA glue or wallpaper paste
- water
- piece of cardboard
- paints
- brushes
- glass jars

1 Cut or tear the paper into small pieces, less than 2 x 4cm/¾ x 1½in in size. If you have a paper shredder, great: shredded newspaper is ideal, and other papers (except shiny types) work well too.

2 In a bucket or bowl, mix some of the glue or paste with enough water to make a thin, creamy consistency.

3 Soak the paper in the glue mixture. Squeeze and squish it into a satisfying soggy mess. Most children will love this!

4 Make four sausage shapes about 15cm/6in long. Take two and bend them into semicircles. Press them on to a base made from a piece of thick cardboard, so they stand up.

5 Shape the other bits to make a shorter tail and a lumpier head and make sure they stand up well too.

6 Leave to dry – this may take several days.

7 Paint to finish.

Papier mâché Timmy the tortoise

Concentrated work for sticky hands, age 6+.

This model makes use of two papier mâché techniques. Both are great for making a mess and getting sticky, which always adds to the fun of creating things together.

You will need

- small mixing bowl
- piece of
- scissors or craft/utility knife
- clear film/plastic wrap
- PVA glue or wallpaper paste
- bucket or large mixing bowl
- water
- scrap paper or newspaper
- masking tape
- paints
- brushes
- glass jars

1 Choose a small bowl to be the mould for the shell. Put it on a piece of cardboard, draw round it, then cut out the circle, trimming off an extra 1cm/½in all round. Put the cardboard on one side.

2 Wrap the outside of the bowl in clear film.

3 Pour some glue into a bucket or mixing

bowl, then add a little water to make it a creamy consistency.

4 Tear the paper into strips measuring about 2 x 7.5cm/¾ x 3in. Drop some of them into the bucket or bowl, allowing them to get thoroughly soaked – get your hands in if you like.

5 Lay the strips in different directions all over the bowl. Keep tearing and adding strips until you have a good thickness of paper (about 3mm/⅛in) over the mould. Leave to dry overnight.

6 To make the head, legs and tail, make papier mâché sausages in the same way as for the Loch Ness Monster. Make four sausages for the legs, a larger one for the head, and a slightly conical one for the tail.

7 Place them and glue in position on the cardboard base you cut out at the start. Leave to dry overnight.

8 Next day, if the papier mâché is dry enough, pull it carefully from the bowl and cling film. Trim the edges and cut some space for the legs, tail and head. Use glue or masking tape to fix the shell to the legs, tail and head that are glued to the carboard.

9 When completely dry, paint to finish.

Funny birds

With this basic method, you and keen little helpers can enjoy transforming old yogurt drink pots, small plastic bottles and cardboard tubes into a lovely menagerie of weird and wonderful birds.

You will need
- white and coloured paper or thin card/stock
- scissors or craft/utility knife
- old yogurt drink pot or similar small plastic bottle
- marker pens and/or crayons
- adhesive tape and/or strong glue
- glue spreader and pot (if using)
- polystyrene ball or ping-pong ball
- wobbly eyes (optional)
- feathers, dyed or natural

1 Cut a rectangle of paper or card long enough to go all the way round the bottle with a small overlap, and wide enough to reach from the bottom to just below the neck.

2 Decorate the paper or card with pens or coloured pencils, if you like.

3 Fix the card on to the body, with tape or glue. Cut a wing shape from the paper or card. Decorate it if you like, and fix it at the back of the body.

4 Cut a foot shape. Fix it on the bottom of the bottle.

Coloured paper

If you haven't got the right coloured paper to hand, paint a sheet of paper. This works best with medium- and heavy-weight paper, and paint of a creamy consistency – poster or acrylic, or household paint. The paper may not dry very flat, but that probably doesn't matter. There's no need to aim for even colour – varied colour usually looks great.

5   Make a triangle of card for a beak. Fix it by cutting a hole for it in the ball (the head) and gluing it, or fixing it with tape if you're using a golf ball.

6   Draw a pair of eyes or stick on wobbly eyes. Tape or glue feathers on to the wings and head.

VARIATION: SNOWMAN

To create this little character, make small cross cuts in the sides of the container and stick in small twigs. Use cloves for eyes. Use a small scrap of fabric for the scarf, and create a hat from a bottle top. And the carrot nose? It's little piece of carrot!

Paper dart

Here's a paper dart that's easy to fold and flies brilliantly. First, make it with an A4/Letter sheet of paper. Later, it's fun to experiment with different sizes, from as tiny as a piece of cigarette paper to a real jumbo jet at A3.

You will need
- rectangular sheet of paper
- ruler
- adhesive tape

1 Fold the paper in half lengthways.
2 Unfold and fold in two of the corners to the middle crease to make two triangles.

3 Fold again, taking the top corners of the triangles over to the middle fold.
4 Fold the dart in half, with the folded triangles on the outside.
5 Create a body for the dart by holding down the ruler and folding back about 1cm/½in from the middle fold on both wings.
6 Stick two pieces of tape on top at the front and the back.
7 Fold two small triangles at the back, turning them up slightly.

YOU'RE READY TO FLY!

If your dart falls too fast, fold small triangles on the wing tips and turn up a little. If it goes up too fast and drops, flatten the triangles and/or add a little weight such as a small piece of thin card/stock in the nose.

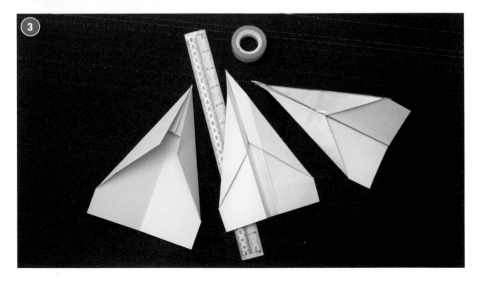

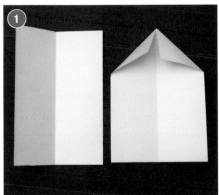

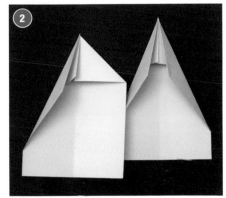

Paper boats

Fun for bath time, in a basin or a paddling pool, these little boats float for a while, and it's easy to make a little fleet of all different sizes.

You will need
- 15cm/6in square or larger piece of paper

1 Fold the square in half. Make a good crease. From both edges, fold into the central fold.

2 Fold in half along the middle fold, with the flaps inside. Turn up a corner from the folded side so that it reaches to about 1cm/½in from the top edge. Repeat on the other end.

3 Make a fold along the top on both sides to make a line a little less than 1cm/½in. Open up the boat.

4 Gently shape the boat. If you pinch the base and make creases on the bottom, it will sit better on the water. Now you're ready to float away.

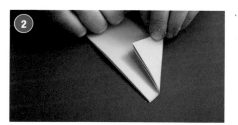

Fairy door and purse

Something to open up a whole new world in your grandchild's imagination.

You will need

- A4/Letter or similar sheet of paper
- scissors and/or craft/utility knife
- adhesive tape
- ruler
- coloured pens/pencils
- Blu Tack

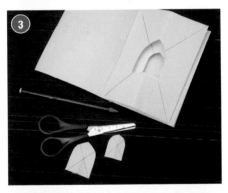

1 Fold the paper in four. Cut a sliver off the top edge. You now have two sheets: secure them with small pieces of tape on the folds to make a kind of book.

2 Draw a door shape on the front page. On the three inner right-hand pages, draw diagonal lines across between the corners with a pencil.

3 Draw another door on each page where the lines intersect, making them smaller each time. On sides two and three, cut out the doors so you can peep through to the next page.

4 Time to decorate the pages! Use your own or your grandchild's drawing skills and imagination for the four pages. Share the action!

5 What shall we draw? Let's make up a story. This could be a magical land with wonderful animals and birds, knights and damsels, dragons and ogres. Create three worlds behind a little magic door.

6 When you've finished, fix the fairy door on a wall somewhere where you can peep at it every now and then. Use a small piece of Blu Tack to hold the pages closed.

Tooth Fairy's purse

Children enjoy keeping secret things in bags and containers. Making tiny envelopes, letters and books is so simple and yet provides a lot of fun and ongoing play. Nowadays, perhaps the Tooth Fairy will need to change her habits in an increasingly cashless society! We'll start here with a credit card.

You will need

- paper or fabric
- scissors or craft/utility knife
- glue stick
- pencil
- credit card

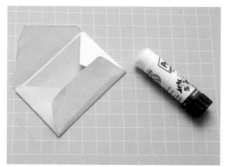

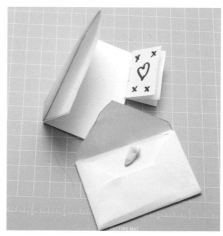

FOR A LITTLE PURSE ENVELOPE

Draw round the credit card. Draw tabs as shown in the photo. Cut out, fold and glue together.

FOR A LITTLE LETTER

Draw round the credit card four times to make a large rectangle. Cut out, fold in half, then cut in half. Fold in half again and trim to fit the envelope.

FOR A LITTLE BOOK

Draw round the credit card. Fold in four. Use a stapler to staple the spine. Trim the edges.

Paper butterflies

You can make a pair of fluttering butterflies in minutes!

You will need

- A4/Letter white or coloured paper coloured pens/pencils
- transparent adhesive tape or masking tape
- scissors
- three 30cm/12in pieces of thick thread

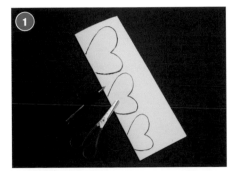

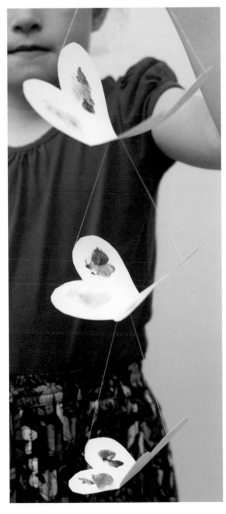

1 Fold the paper in half along its length. Draw half a butterfly shape three times.
2 Cut each of them out and you'll have three butterflies to colour in.
3 Tape the thread either side to the underside of the wings, about 1cm/½in from the edges and 3cm/1in from the top. Now, if you lift the thread up and down, your pretty butterflies will come to life!

Taking things apart

You'll know the good rule: if it ain't broke, don't fix it. Another one is that if it *is* broken, and can't be mended, don't throw it away – take it apart, with a little helper, probably aged over 6.

Next time someone kills a kettle by boiling it dry too many times, don't get too hot and bothered: once you've cooled down, it's an opportunity as much as a problem!

If you have one of those cases of tools that contains every size and shape of screwdriver imaginable, now's your chance to try out some of the ones you've never used before.

Let the child at your side do as much as possible. The aim is simply to learn how to dismantle something and see what's inside. There's no need to worry about putting anything back together again.

Interesting components

You'll find plenty of interesting bits to store away for model making later. You may discover a coil of copper wire that's like treasure to a child. Loudspeakers can reveal magnets. Printed circuit boards look lovely on a home-made spaceship. Coloured wires can decorate a home-made robot. And you'll build up a nice collection of useful small screws.

If the child at your side is interested, and you know enough, you can make it an engineering or electronics lesson. And whatever your knowledge, you can both simply enjoy looking at and wondering what the various bits do.

Items that are great to take apart include: kitchen and bathroom scales, old clocks, clockwork kitchen timers, CD and

DVD players, loudspeakers, vacuum cleaners, computer keyboards, lawn mowers, hair dryers, toasters and kettles.

'What's this for, Grandad?'

Whether or not you have any idea what this or that component is for, it can be fun to go online and try to work it out with the child at your side. There are several spectacular electronic components catalogues online where you see hundreds of items ... look and learn!

Really yummy stuff – simple fun with cooking

Two kitchen rules when cooking with kids

MURPHY'S LAW
If things can go wrong, they will go wrong. So have aprons, cloths, towels and easy-to-wipe-clean surfaces all at the ready.

DON'T BE IN A HURRY
It spoils the fun, and can spoil the food. Find as many tasks as possible that the children at your side can participate in, or do by themselves.

Personalised pizzas
Suitable for children aged 3+

Children love to have choices: here they can make entirely personalised pizzas. Their choices may be strange; let them find out what combinations work best for them.

You can start with a ready-made plain pizza base (if so, jump down to decorating the pizzas, below) or spend extra fun time together making them from scratch. Children particularly enjoy this as it's an excuse to get their hands very sticky.

Makes: 4 small pizzas
Prep time: about 30 minutes
Cooking time: 15–20 minutes

You will need

- about 100g/8 tbsp self-raising/self-rising flour, plus extra for dusting
- 4 pinches each of salt and ground black pepper
- 60ml/4 tbsp sunflower oil
- about 90ml/6 tbsp warm water
- 60ml/4 tbsp tomato puree or 1 can tinned chopped tomatoes, drained
- other toppings, see box
- extra grated Cheddar, Red Leicester or Double Gloucester cheese
- olive oil, for drizzling

You will also need

- large mixing bowl
- wooden spoon
- rolling pin
- fork
- 2 frying pans
- 2 baking trayscutting board
- knife
- oven gloves

1. Preheat the oven to 220°C/200°C fan/425°F/Gas 7.

2. Put the flour and seasoning into a large mixing bowl. Stir in the oil and enough warm water to bring the mixture together to form a ball. Add a little extra water to get the dough nicely pliable, or more flour if it's too sticky.

3. Knead the dough on a floured work surface for a couple of minutes, so it is slightly springy. (It can be split in two: children can help by squeezing and rolling smaller lumps, pushing them together with the heel of their hand.)

4. Roll the dough out to make four very thin discs about 15cm/6in in diameter and about 3mm/⅛thin thick. Prick them all over with a fork.

5 Place both frying pans over medium-high heat. Place a dough disc on each and cook for about 4 minutes: it should be starting to brown underneath. Turn over and repeat.

6 Remove the pizza bases and place on the floured work surface. Cook the next two discs in the same way. Allow all four to cool a little.

7 Spread the tomato puree or tinned chopped tomatoes all over each disc, leaving a border round the edge of about 1cm/½in.

8 Now it's time to personalise your pizzas. See the box for topping ideas.

DECORATING THE PIZZAS

9 After everyone has placed their selection of toppings on the pizzas, drizzle a little oil all over. You can also grate some extra cheese all over it, if your helpers like it, perhaps mild or mature/sharp Cheddar, and – for extra colour – Red Leicester or Double Gloucester.

10 Place the pizzas on baking trays in the oven. Bake for 8 minutes, then check them. Are the crusts nice and golden? If not, leave in for a couple more minutes.

11 Take them out of the oven, and allow them to cool slightly before serving.

'What can I put on my pizza, Grandad?'

What's in your kitchen? An interesting variety? If you are lucky, they might try something new from:

- corn – canned or sliced baby corn
- sausages – sliced pork or vegetarian ones, or sliced chorizo or salami
- ham and bacon – cut into small pieces
- olives – pitted/stoned, whole or halved
- mushrooms – wiped clean and sliced
- bell peppers – seeded and sliced
- spinach – rinsed small leaves
- pineapple – drained canned chunks or fresh pieces
- tomatoes – halved baby ones or sliced larger ones courgettes/zucchini – cut into 1cm/½in cubes
- broccoli – cut into tiny florets
- sweet potato – cut into 1cm/½in cubes
- butternut squash – flesh cut into 1cm/½in cubes
- cheeses – mozzarella or Cheddar, cut into thin slices or grated

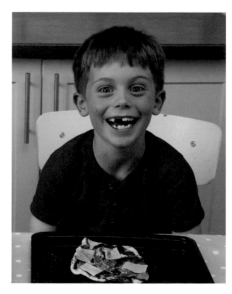

Magic toast

Suitable for children aged 3+
Children find this fun, funny and tasty.

Makes: as much as you like!
Prep time: about 2 minutes
Cooking time: 2 minutes

You will need
- thick sliced bread
- butter or margarine
- honey, jam/jelly, Marmite or peanut butter

You will also need
- sharp knife

1 It's very simple. Make some toast with thick sliced bread.
2 Cut it into two halves, then take a very sharp knife and cut between the toast's two sides to make a kind of pocket.

3 Spread some butter or margarine in the pocket space, then spread your chosen filling inside. Close up the pocket.
4 Pretend you are giving them plain toast with nothing on it. Children love the joke and like to keep up the pretence with others. And it does actually taste more exciting than normal toast!

Potato boats

These are popular with young pirates and landlubbers of all ages…

Makes: 4
Prep time: about 15 minutes
Cooking time: 45 minutes

You will need
- Cheddar cheese
- 2 medium-size baking potatoes
- can of tomato soup

You will also need
- baking tray
- small pan
- oven gloves
- bowls or plates

1 Preheat the oven to 200°C/180°C fan/400°F/gas 6.

2 Cut some slices of cheese, about 3–5mm/1/8–1/4in thick and 10cm/4in square. Cut these in half to make triangles.

3 Cut the potatoes in half lengthways. Cut a little slice off their bottoms so they sit flat. Place them on a baking tray, put them in the oven and bake for about 45 minutes, until cooked through.

4 After about 40 minutes, pour the soup into the pan. Heat it up, but do not let it boil.

5 Take the potatoes out and check if they're ready by taking a sharp knife and sticking it into a potato. If it goes in easily, it's probably done. If there's resistance, give them a few more minutes.

6 Take the potatoes out and put them on four bowls or plates. Leave to cool a bit.

7 Cut a slit in the top of each potato half. Insert the cheese triangles. Pour the soup around the potatoes. Now your boats are ready to set sail – and hopefully you'll see them go down fast!

Funny fruit faces

Suitable for children aged 2½–12.
Older children can learn to do it all without
any help or supervision.

Serves: **4**
Prep time: **about 10 minutes**

You will need
- packet of Angel Delight or similar firm-setting milk pudding (or make small bowls of jelly some hours in advance)
- satsumas – separate segments
- bananas – cut in discs
- grapes – cut in half
- currants or sultanas/golden raisins
- dried apricots – cut in half
- optional naughty extra: squirty cream

You will also need
- measuring jug/cup
- mixing bowl
- whisk
- 4 small bowls

1 Make up the milk pudding according to the packet instructions: usually, it involves putting 300ml/½ pint/1¼ cups dairy or other milk into a bowl and whisking in the contents of the packet.
2 Pour into four small bowls. Leave for a few minutes to set.
3 Now make funny faces using your fruits.

Chocolate cake

Suitable for children aged 3+.
Not only is this very tasty cake a top choice
with children, it also provides extra interest
as they can choose different ingredients
and experiment with them.

Serves: 8–12, depending on greed!
Prep time: about 25 minutes
Cooking time: 45 minutes

You will need
For the cake
- 175g/6oz soft baking margarine or butter, plus
  extra for greasing
- 175g/6oz sugar
- 3 large/US extra large eggs, lightly beaten
- 175g/6oz self-raising/self-rising flour
- 30ml/2 tbsp each of any two of the following:
- treacle/molasses – for a darker flavour
- malt extract – for a more toffee-like flavour
- honey – for a … erm … honey flavour
- golden/light corn syrup – for extra
  sweetness
- chocolate hazelnut spread – for a slightly nutty
  flavour

- chocolate drops – for a crunchy cake
- 100g/3¾oz/generous ¾ cup unsweetened
  cocoa powder
- 5ml/1 tsp vanilla extract (optional)

For the filling and icing
- ½ jar apricot jam/jelly
- 175g/6oz icing/confectioners' sugar, sifted
- 100g/4oz/6 tbsp unsweetened cocoa powder,
  sifted
- hazelnut-sized lump of butter or soft baking
  margarine
- 60ml/4 tbsp hot water
- 10ml/2 tsp treacle/molasses or golden/light
  corn syrup or chocolate/hazelnut spread

You will also need
- 2 sandwich cake tins/pans about 18cm/7in
  diameter, preferably with loose bases
- baking parchment
- mixing bowls
- wooden spoon or electric mixer
- spatula
- sharp knife or skewer
- wire rack
- wide, flat knife or angled spatula

1 Preheat the oven to 180°C/160°C fan/350°F/Gas 4.
2 Grease the tins, then line with baking parchment.
3 Cream the margarine or butter and the sugar in a large mixing bowl with a wooden spoon or electric mixer.
4 Gradually beat in the eggs (or for a vegan alternative, see Variation), alternating with spoonfuls of flour to prevent curdling. Add the selected extra ingredients, then mix again.
5 Sift in the flour, bicarbonate of soda and cocoa, then fold in to combine. It should be a soft dropping consistency; if not, add a little more flour or some milk.
6 Transfer the mixture into the tins. Spread out evenly with a spatula. Place in the middle of the oven and bake for 20 minutes.
7 To check if the cake is cooked, stick a sharp knife or skewer into the middle: if it comes out clean, it's ready. If not, return the cake to the oven for a few minutes more.
8 Remove from the oven and leave to cool for a few minutes in the tins, then transfer to a wire rack to cool completely.
9 To fill the cake, spread the jam generously on one half of the cake, then place the other half on top.
10 To make the icing, sift the icing sugar and cocoa into a large mixing bowl. Add the fat and hot water. Mix well. Add a little more water or icing sugar, and beat to get a stiff silky mixture. Add your chosen flavouring.
11 Put the icing on top of the cake, in a great blob in the middle. Using a wide, flat knife or angled spatula, spread it out. It is easier to move the cake around clockwise or anticlockwise rather than moving your hand around.
12 Leave to set for about an hour.

VEGAN VARIATION
For a vegan alternative, replace the eggs with 15ml/1 tbsp cider vinegar plus 15ml/1tsp bicarbonate of soda, mixed with 200ml/7fl oz/scant 1 cup dairy-free milk and leave for a few minutes before using. Use margarine in place of butter.

Great things to make and do outdoors

Family walks and other outdoor activities often become treasured milestones in children's memories. Some well judged and well timed adult input can turn a good day into a brilliant one.

Some children have good sticking power. Some need more encouragement to get more enjoyment. So, want to spice a park or woodland walk? You can easily add extra excitement and fun with these activities – whether on a walk, waiting around for a bus, or stuck in the car. Time need not drag with Grandad around!

Outdoor fun and games

Camouflage
- For 1 or more children aged 3+
- with one adult

You walk through a wood, chatting to the child or children. Take a bit of time, and enjoy the conversation. They have to pay attention and stay close, and they must listen out for the signal: as soon as you slip the word 'camouflage' into the conversation, they have to run off. You count down (without looking) from 20 to zero, loudly. They have to be ready by the time you call out zero, whereupon they have to freeze.

They are aiming to be as well camouflaged as possible. This can mean hiding in bushes, wrapping themselves around branches, hiding behind a signpost, burying themselves in leaves. You try to find them: in the case of very

young ones, pretending you can't see them; in the case of older ones, possibly being completely flummoxed as to where they are.

Mysterious mounds
- This is fun for children (probably age 5+) to do entirely on their own

The idea is simply to leave some trace of your visit using sticks, stones or any other natural debris. It could be a mound of stones. It could be pictures on the ground made of sticks. The only restriction is not to use any living material.

It's fun to think that someone will walk by and not notice your mound, or that someone else may spot it and wonder who made it. You could come back after a week and see if man or nature has made a mark on your creation.

Forty Forty, or Pom Pom

- 3 or more players, aged 4+

This game is best played in woodland or parks where you have some open space, occasional bushes and trees, and also on beaches where there are few people and lots of rocks to hide behind.

Choose a tree or rock as base. The person who is 'on' counts slowly to 40. The others hide. Their aim is to creep back unnoticed. As soon as the seeker has spotted someone hiding or running back, he shouts: 'Forty Forty I see...' (and names the person), then dashes back to base. At the same time, the person who's been spotted tries to get back first, shouting: 'Forty Forty home' if he succeeds. If he doesn't get there first, he has to stay there, in prison.

It's not great if the person who is 'on' hangs around the base for long. The best games are ones when he moves away from base, enticing people to break cover.

The game is over when everyone has reached safety or been caught. In one version of the game, someone getting home uncaught can release the prisoners (shouting: 'Forty Forty release') and they can all go off again.

Statues

- Suitable for children aged 3+
- 3 or more players

Can they stay still for 20 seconds? It's a big ask for some little ones! This works especially well if there are seats, tables or logs to climb on. Each child takes up a pose and has to hold it for a slow count of 20. You can ask for particular poses: everyone be sad, be happy, be angry, be like a tree, be like a squirrel, and so on. They can hold a prop, such as a branch of leaves. You can award points. Take photos if you like. Then move on to another spot a few minutes' walking distance away.

Treasure hunt

- Suitable for children aged 18 months+
- any number of players

There can be lots of interesting things to find on walks. Send out treasure hunters to look for things such as six different leaves, four round pebbles and jagged stones (see also page 96 'On the beach').

Seadog Simon Says

- Suitable for children aged 4+
- 3 or more players

This is an energetic version of Simon Says, especially for young pirates. In the original game, the person who is Simon gives a command and everyone must do it if the command is preceded by the words 'Simon says'; if not, the others mustn't do the action. It's fun for even very young children.

Here, Seadog Simon says what the captain's orders are. If they say: 'Captain's orders … scrub the deck', you have to do it. But if they don't say: 'Captain's orders' before giving the command, you stay quite still! Here are some orders; you can add others. You will have to explain them to the crew first:

'Scrub the decks!' (Go on all fours and pretend to scrub the ground.)

'Up the crow's nest!' (Pretend to climb rigging.)

'Pipe 'em up!' (Pretend to blow a whistle, make a whistling noise.)

'Hard to port!' (Everyone rush to their left.)

'Hard to starboard!' (Everyone rush to their right.)

'Turn about!' (Everyone turns round.)

Take it in turns to be Seadog Simon. You can play the game so someone ends up as the winner. You are out of the game if you are spotted making two mistakes.

Grandad's Footsteps

- Suitable for children aged 3+
- 3 or more players

This game is better known as Grandmother's Footsteps, but we're going for equal opportunities here... One person is 'it': the rest try to creep up unnoticed. The person who is 'it' stands with their back facing the others, who start about 20 paces or more away and try to creep up. The person who's 'it' stays still, then turns around suddenly to see if anyone is moving. If they spot anyone, they call the name out, and that person goes back to the starting line. Anyone who manages to touch the one who's 'it' takes over.

What's the Time Mr Wolf?

- Suitable for children aged 3+
- 3 or more players

Similar to Grandad's Footsteps, this is another all-time favourite. Children ask: 'What's the time Mr Wolf?' and he replies: 'ten o'clock' or whatever, and they creep up. They keep asking, until he suddenly says: 'dinner time!' and chases everyone all over the place.

Waiting games

Maybe you're waiting in a queue. Maybe you have the joy of grandchildren with you on a car or train journey. Or the service in a cafe is rather slow and everyone is hungry and getting fractious. Whatever the situation, it's always useful to have a few ideas up your sleeve to fill some time. Whisk out some of these to add froth and fun!

'Grandad, I'm bored. Are we nearly there yet?'

Quiet in the Jungle
- Suitable for children aged 3–10
- 2 or more players

Smaller children especially love this. It's a great way to get them quiet, and it's funny for all players.

To play, the leader says the magic words:

'Quiet in the jungle,
Quiet in the street,
The biggest fattest monkey
Is about to speak.'

At which point, everyone has to be quiet for as long as possible. When eventually somebody makes a noise by accident (or by accident-on-purpose) they're the monkey, and everyone laughs! And you do it again … and again.

Thingy bidding

- Suitable for children aged about 4+
- 2 or more players plus a leader (you can also play in pairs who can confer)

This is a competitive word game that can be made dead easy for little ones or really difficult for big ones.

It's about subjects or categories, best described for younger minds as 'things' or 'thingies'. The leader sets a thingy challenge: 'How many words can you find for...' and names some thingy. These can be easy or hard, general or precise, chosen to suit the players. For example, colours, or types of car, or vegetables, or Leeds City goalies.

Each player has a few seconds to think of as many as possible, and quickly makes a bid for the subject. Four? Five? Six? How many?! The person with the highest bid has to deliver all the words. If you do, you win a point. If not, you lose a point. Continue playing for five rounds or until everyone is tired.

Yes-No Game

- Suitable for children aged about 3+
- 2 players

Here's another golden oldie that never ceases to delight children. Player one starts as the questioner. Their aim is to get the other player to answer a question by saying 'yes' or 'no', while player two has to find answers to all the questions without saying either 'yes' or 'no'. For example:

Q: 'Is your name John?'
A: 'It is.'
Q: 'Do you like that name?'
A: 'I would prefer to be called Zac.'

The trick is for the questioner not just to ask closed questions (ones normally answered with a 'yes' or 'no'), but also to ask open questions (ones that require all sorts of answers) and then slip in a closed question when their opponent's guard is down!

Number Plate Bingo

- Suitable for children aged about 5+
- 2 or more players plus a caller

You will need

- pencils
- paper

Any young children who know their alphabet can take part. Each player draws a three-by-three grid (like for noughts and crosses/tic-tac-toe) and writes in nine random letters, excluding I and Q. The caller (probably a front passenger) calls out the last letter on a car number/licence plate he can see. When a player has a full row of letters crossed off, he shouts 'bingo'. Players make new cards for themselves and start again.

Smelly Substitutes

- Suitable for children aged 7+
- 2 or more players

For some strange reason, small boys in particular find this game hilarious. First, you have to know what a verb or a 'doing word' is, or learn about it. Then the oldest player thinks of a verb and some sentences with it in. You might want to use pen and paper to help think things through.

Now, say the sentences out loud, but replace the verb with the word 'smell'. The other players have to work out what the hidden verb is. The person who guesses first plays next, or the game goes round clockwise.

For example: 'I smell in the garden.' 'I smell down the road.' 'I smell to school.' 'Grandad likes to smell by the sea.'

The 'Oo' Game

- Suitable for children aged about 6+
- 2 or more players

This is a silly game that takes a little practice. The aim is to find an 'oo' word. What's an 'oo' word, I hear you ask? English has many: words that either contain two os or other letters that make the sound 'oo', such as 'flu' or 'juice'.

    Player one says a word that isn't an 'oo' word. Player two has to think of a word that is connected in some way to the first one. If possible, this should be an 'oo' word. Play continues until someone finds a word that is both connected and an 'oo' word. Players may challenge the connection: if the other players think the

connection isn't good enough, play continues. Connections can be all sorts of things, including opposites.

    Once someone wins a round with an 'oo' word, play can continue for as many more rounds as people like.

    Two examples:

    'Bed ... sleep ... night ... moon!'

    'Butterfly ... nectar ... flower ... blue!'

On the beach

Donkey

- Suitable for children aged 4+
- 2 or more players

Stand in a circle and throw a ball from one person to another clockwise. When a player misses the ball they become 'D'. Second time they miss, they're 'D-O', and so on until they spell out 'D-O-N-K-E-Y', and then they're out.

Beachcombing treasure hunt

- Suitable for children aged 4+
- 1 or more players

Set the kids a challenge. Give them a long or short shopping list (depending on their age and independence). Remember, younger children are typically quite unobservant, so they'll need help. Write a list or just tell them one category at a time: 'Find me':

'one flat stone'
'two stones with stripes in them'
'three feathers'
'four different shells'
'five pieces of seaweed'
… and so on.

When your treasure hunters have finished, get them to lay out the spoils neatly on the sand. You might have prizes ready, or you may find they simply want to do another treasure hunt. The best-presented collection can win first prize, everyone else gets second prize. Don't necessarily be the judge yourself – it's better to encourage the youngsters to use their own critical faculties, so get each of them to say which they think is best and why. When all's done, why not help set up a little museum at home with the treasures?

Penalty Catch

- Suitable for children aged 5+
- 2 or more players

Stand a few strides apart in a circle and throw a ball to one another clockwise. Each time you drop a catch there's a penalty:

> first drop: go down on one knee
> second drop: go down on both knees
> third drop: put one hand behind the back
> fourth drop: close one eye
> fifth drop: both hands behind the back (you have to try to catch with your chin!)
> sixth drop: you're out

In one version, penalties can be cancelled when you make a successful catch – for example, going back from kneeling on one knee to standing if you catch once after having dropped once.

Two useful hints for a great day

The best time to bathe?

On many beaches, the best time to bathe is when the tide is coming in over sand that's been warmed by the sun during the afternoon. Many visitors start to leave busy beaches in the afternoon and miss the best bathing!

Watch the wind.

If you have a choice of beaches, check local weather information to see which way and how strong the wind is blowing. Why? First, you can choose one that will be more sheltered. Second, you can choose one that may have more surf (winds coming in from the sea can help make surf stronger). And third, you can avoid a beach that will have a mini-sandstorm and give you extra sand in your sandwiches.

Hunting for sea life

- Suitable for children aged 1+

Any beach or shore is teeming with masses of life – if you know where to look. Apart from rock pools, don't forget to look carefully under rocks at the water's edge at mid to low tide. There's a good chance of finding crabs, small fish and sometimes a starfish.

Very low tides are particularly good for looking at sea life: if you go down to the low-tide margins you will often see far more sea creatures than at other times; search round rocks and seaweed for shrimps, crabs and small fish.

USEFUL THINGS TO TAKE

- Crablines – very cheap, and well worth buying for hours of fun. Warn your children to watch out for the hooks, then wait for them to learn the lesson when, like everyone else, they get a hook stuck in a finger! Hanging crablines over quays, rocks and in rock pools can produce great results – crabs, fish, shrimps, even starfish. Keep still and wait.
- A brightly coloured net – less easy to lose – preferably with a strong frame. Sea life seems unfazed by lurid colours.
- A good-sized household plastic bucket – seaside buckets tend to be too small if you catch anything large.
- A clear measuring jug/cup – this will enable

Looking after captives

Ensure that whatever your grandchildren catch is kept safe from harm in a bucket of water while they examine it. The bucket should contain seaweed and rocks for the captured fish and other creatures to hide under. Keep it covered or in a shaded spot: if the water becomes too warm it loses much of its oxygen, and your captives may suffocate.

Keep an eye on what's put into the bucket – it's upsetting for a child to discover that some of their prize catch has been eaten by another of their captives! Crabs can be villains. Be sure to release everything live back into a rock pool before you leave.

your grandchild to get a better look at little sea creatures.

- A magnifying glass.
- A glass jar, for small shells that can otherwise easily get lost.

Topshells – pretty and numerous

Easily found around and under rocks, sometimes in huge numbers. They get their name from being quite like a spinning top. Their grey or mauve chequered patterns are well worth looking at closely with a magnifying glass.

Periwinkles – sea snails happy out of water

The largest type of periwinkle in the UK is the edible periwinkle, which is up to 3cm/1¼in wide. Smaller ones tend to take the colour of their surroundings as camouflage, and are often orange or yellow. They can survive out of seawater for weeks.

Mussels – pretty morsels on the rocks

Shiny black mussels are unmistakable. Their shells make excellent decorations for sand castles. Smaller ones sometimes cover large areas of the rocks found between high and low water. The larger ones – best for eating – usually stay underwater.

Whelks – vampires on the rocks!

Periwinkles and topshells graze peacefully on seaweeds. Not so whelks – they're hunters, vampires even, most often found lurking under lower-shore rocks. They prey on barnacles and mussels, boring into the shell, sticking in an appendage that's like an elephant's trunk and a rasp, and then sucking out the juices and scraping out the tastiest bits of their victim.

Razor shells – sharp but shy

You won't often see a live razor shell because usually it will have buried itself deep in the sand while the tide is out. If you tread on a live one, or just a shell, you'll know about it, as they're very sharp.

Mermaid's purse – coolest egg box ever

Mermaid's purses are egg cases of the dogfish, a small shark common around the UK. At each corner there's a tendril that works its way around seaweed, anchoring the purse. Each egg case holds one egg, from which the baby shark emerges, leaving an empty case. You might find one washed up on the high-water mark. They're a real treasure for taking home.

Cockles – tasty little number

Common cockles have very distinctive shells, frequently found on sandy beaches. Dig down and you may find live ones. Birds and people alike find them very tasty.

Star barnacles – lunar landscape on the rocks

There are millions of these on seashore rocks, but we hardly notice them. Get a magnifying glass and take a look. They look like something out of a sci-fi story. When underwater, the middle section opens up like a trapdoor, and the barnacle flicks out special feathery legs to bring tiny particles of food to its mouth.

Wrack – bubble and pop seaweed

There are various types of wrack. They usually have little lumps like small eggs or peanuts. These are gas bladders that enable the plant to stand upright when the tide is in so that they can get more light. Its other name is popweed, and it's fun for children to pop the bladders.

Anemones – loads of tentacles but armless

There are many anemones. The beadlet anemone is a reddish jelly-like blob stuck to rocks. If you can find a snakelock anemone with tentacles waving in a pool, be sure to get your grandchild to hold a finger close to it so that they can feel it nibbling them.

Shrimps and prawns – complex characters

The brown shrimp is mottled grey or brown, excellent camouflage on sandy surfaces. There are various types of prawn, mostly semi-transparent. Always on the search for food, they're great fun to observe in rock pools and buckets. Watch out for the funny way they shoot away backwards.

They are extraordinary, very complex compared to the little piece of them that some of us get to eat! They have a pair of antennules, for balance; a pair of antennae, which are sensory organs; six pairs of limbs around the mouth, including biting jaws and limbs to hold food; maxillae, which pump water over the gills; four pairs of walking legs; and five pairs of limbs for swimming.

How tasty are you?

Fancy being nibbled by a prawn or shrimp? Search rockpools: if you hold still enough and are patient, one may pop out and delicately nibble at your fingertips, taking microscopic bits of dead skin. Yummy!

Birdwatching

Birdwatching is fun, but for most children just *looking* at something isn't very exciting. Pick out some interesting facts, though, and things start to come to life. The birds here are all relatively easy to spot. Most are resident in large areas of the UK all year round.

Magpie – villain in the woods!

Magpies are hunters and scavengers, often seen eating carrion on the road. They have a distinctive loopy flight, with a long tail acting as a rudder. Look out for their deep black and bright white feathers on walks. Listen for their 'chack chack' and chuckling sounds. You can also often tell when a magpie is around: smaller birds set up a chorus of alarm calls – danger! Magpies steal eggs, and attack not only baby birds but occasionally also larger targets, such as rabbits, lambs and even adult sheep.

Mute swan – feathered jumbo jet!

Watch the adults puff up their wings in defence, looking rather like a galleon. Like jumbo jets, swans need a very long take-off; they can't take off on land, but need a long, clear runway on water. Immature swans are dappled brown or dull grey, before their plumage gradually changes to white. Remember to tell the story of the ugly duckling!

Robin Redbreast – friendliest of birds

He actually has an orange, not red, breast and face. Listen out for his sharp 'tik' alarm call, and his high-pitched warbling song. He's very friendly. He'll suddenly appear from nowhere, especially when you dig in the garden or have a picnic. Sit still, and he might hop up next to you.

Buzzard – high-flying hunter

Sailing far up high, they may look small, but these are huge hunters. Hold your arms out wide: that'll give your grandchild an idea of the wingspan. Buzzards are often seen leisurely circling high up, alone or in pairs, catching thermal currents. Listen for a call like the mewing of a cat. And look out for an attack from smaller birds: it's common to see them flying around a buzzard like little Spitfires attacking a great big bomber, annoying the big bird and seeing it off decisively.

Kestrel – look out on a car journey

This is the only commonly seen British bird that hovers. It heads into the wind, spreads its tail in a fan shape and flaps its sharp pointed wings lightly, almost motionless as it hovers looking for small rodents. Green scrubland by roads and motorways provides good hunting ground: you can quite often see them hovering above the road on a car journey.

Mandarin duck – a beautiful immigrant

This spectacular bird originally came from the Far East centuries ago and is now a common sight on many lakes and ponds in the UK. It's the males who'd win a beauty contest, with orange plumes on their cheeks, orange 'sails' on their back, and pale orange sides; the females are dull in comparison, with grey heads, brown backs and white stripes by the eyes.

Sky at night

Look – it's amazing! On a clear night, you can see planets millions of miles away, stars trillions of years in the past. Introduce a grandchild to the wonders of the universe.

Stargazing is complicated. Share the wonder by keeping things simple, and tell a story. For example, explain that constellations are groups of stars that make pictures that thousands of years ago people gave names to, because they thought they were gods, goddesses and heavenly animals.

Getting started

In many places, light pollution can make it hard to spot all but the brightest lights in the sky. The ones here are amongst the easiest to see anywhere.

For maximum enjoyment, allow lots of time for people's eyes to become accustomed to the dark, at least 10 minutes. You'll see stars much better. Cover your phone or torch with red cellophane to mute the light. You could lie on the ground, maybe wrapped in a blanket. Have everyone shut their eyes for a long time. Fill the time with fun things: for example, get everyone counting to a

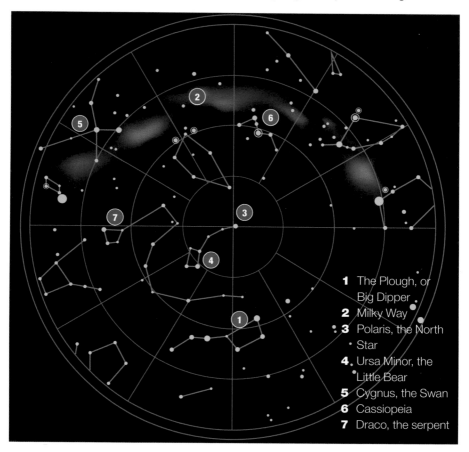

1 The Plough, or Big Dipper
2 Milky Way
3 Polaris, the North Star
4 Ursa Minor, the Little Bear
5 Cygnus, the Swan
6 Cassiopeia
7 Draco, the serpent

hundred several times; do some times tables; play some word games. Take the opportunity to chat with eyes shut. Then open your eyes and – wow – what a sight!

Easy to spot constellations

The diagram of the night sky (left) is simplified: it misses out millions of stars! But it does pick out seven relatively easy-to-spot constellations as seen from the Northern Hemisphere.

At most times of year, you can get your bearings by spotting the Plough. Turn the diagram around to match its position, and you may find your way round to the others.

Great things to see
MOON – A NEARBY FRIENDLY FACE

That's at least one thing that's easy to spot. It looks large because it is relatively

close to earth. The moon appears to change size as days go by, because of the shadow the earth casts on it. Unlike stars, the moon has no light of its own. At full moon, the earth casts no shadow, so it looks large. At new moon it's all in shadow. The moon waxes (grows) and wanes (diminishes): if the crescent appears to face left the moon is getting larger: if it faces right it's reducing.

PLANETS

See a very bright light in the sky? It's probably a planet. They change position and are visible only at some times of year. Check for information online such as BBC websites or in print media. Brightest is Venus (the goddess of love), sometimes very clear just before sunrise and at dusk. Jupiter (king of the gods) appears as a bright yellowish white point of light. Saturn (god of farming) is bright yellow. (Its famous rings are only visible through a telescope.)

STARS

Some of the brightest stars are shown in the diagram. Children will like to find the one with a funny name – often pronounced Beetlejuice – which is much brighter and roughly 1,000 times the size of our sun, only much, much farther way.

Locating things in the sky

It can be hard to show children where to look. Try directing via landmarks at sunset – 'you see that church tower, move your eyes up from there and then this way'. Or start your directions from the moon.

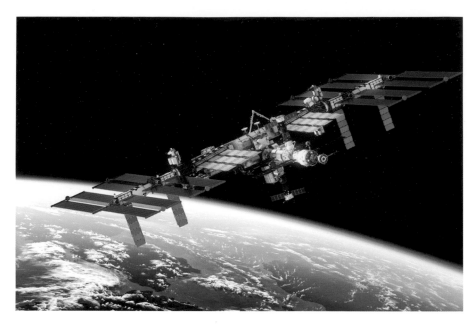

SPACE STATIONS AND SATELLITES
Look out for small lights flashing faster than planes – sometimes moving slowly, sometimes fast across the sky.

THE MILKY WAY
Away from towns, this can be very clear on some nights, You'll see a huge band of what looks like a cloud but is actually more than 100 billion stars, whose light has taken more than 20,000 years to reach us!

POLARIS – THE NORTH STAR
Used for centuries by sailors for navigation. Often fairly easy to spot, Polaris is the only star that appears to stay in the same place in the sky. Use a compass to find north, and look up; or note where the sun sets (due west) and look 90 degrees to the right and upwards. Near Polaris you may see five stars that make a kind of box, with Polaris as a kind of handle. They make up Ursa Minor (the Little Bear).

CYGNUS – THE SWAN
See if you can make out distinctive wings or a cross shape – this constellation is also called the Northern Cross.

CASSIOPEIA
Named after a Greek queen – look for a distinctive W or M shape.

Big numbers!

If you have a grandchild who's interested in numbers, they may like to know a little about the very big numbers in space. For example, the sun is about 91 million miles/146.5 million km away. Sirius is about 9 light years away – that's more than 54 trillion miles – 54,000,000,000,000 miles (or 87 trillion km)! And Polaris is 430 light years away – that's an awful lot more noughts ... got pen and paper to work it out?

Cygnus

Polaris

Little bear

The plough

THE PLOUGH OR BIG DIPPER

Very distinctive at some times of year, the Plough looks like a pan in the sky. It sits just under the Little Bear.

ORION – THE MIGHTY HUNTER

A great archer in Greek mythology, Orion is often the easiest constellation to spot by picking out three distinctive bright stars that make his belt. Then you may be able to make out the rest of him.

Harry Potter stars

Harry Potter fans will like to know that several characters are named after stars in the sky at night. For example:

- **Sirius** – the brightest star in the sky, also called the Dog Star, part of the constellation Canis Major, the Great Dog. Find Sirius near Orion's belt to the left, usually a bluish white.
- **Bellatrix** – she's on Orion's arm, ready to shoot deadly arrows.
- **Draco** – a man-eating serpent. Quite difficult to spot, sometimes visible lurking near the horizon, more easily seen in warmer months.

Betelgeuse

Bellatrix

Orion's belt

Out and about in parks, woodland and countryside

You don't need to be an expert to open a child's eyes to the wonders and pleasures of nature. What's more, kids have a natural excitement and inquisitiveness that we as adults often lose: walking with children can be just as much an eye-opener for an adult!

Some useful things to take

You don't need any equipment for a good time out, but these items can come in handy:

- a groundsheet or old blanket to lie on
- paintbrush to pick up insects
- white plastic container – old ice-cream or margarine pot to help see them, and something for them to hide in, such as an old envelope

- magnifying glass
- toilet paper, for cleaning up a cardboard tube
- bottles of water, to drink, for washing hands, and cleaning wounds and specimens
- magnifying glass
- glass jar
- sticking plasters/Band-Aids and antiseptic wipes/cream

Sensational observations!

The great outdoors provides excellent opportunities for interesting observations. If you focus on a specific sense, it will catch a child's interest and imagination. Their senses are often more acute than adults'.

WHAT CAN YOU HEAR?

Choose a good time to get your group really quiet. All stand still, or lie on the ground. Play a couple of rounds of Quiet in the Jungle (on page 92). When the game is over, take time enjoying the peace and quiet. Then get everyone to WHISPER things they can hear. Creaking trees; rustling grass; buzzing insects; the wind in leaves and branches; a tractor in a field.

WHAT CAN YOU SMELL?

Lie on the ground, or sniff around a small area pretending to be a dog: you can pick up interesting woodland scents, such as woody smells, decaying smells, flowery smells, moist smells, earthy smells, dry and new leaves. Many plants have their own recognisable smells; keep your nose open for wild herbs such as mint and garlic; in chalky areas, there may be wild oregano, marjoram and thyme. Their scents may vary with the season, too. For example, a sycamore leaf in autumn smells like brown sugar; quite different from its spring smell.

WHAT CAN YOU SEE?

First, lie on the ground on your back, then stare up at the trees. Now go on all fours like an animal and look around. Finally, look through a cardboard tube. These three ways of looking can help you focus on different things. When you're on your back, you appreciate something of the tree canopy. On your knees, you start to see the woods from an animal's perspective. Using the tube helps you focus on particular things.

WHAT CAN YOU FEEL?

Stroke trees and feel how different some barks are. Stroke some leaves and feel how some are smooth and some are rasping. Find some feathers and stroke them – some are firm and some are fluffy. Try tickling them under your chin!

WHAT CAN YOU FIND?

Children usually like to hunt for things. You may have to show a very young child first, and go round with them, but after that they may manage by themselves for the next hunt.

Set a challenge to find various things. For example, for a very young child, keep things simple: ask for a thin twig and a bigger one; a green leaf and a brown leaf; a thin blade of grass and a wide one; two feathers; a round stone and a sharp stone. For older children, you could ask for four different leaves, feathers, stones and pinecones.

Dead wood is full of life. Much of woodland wildlife relies on dead wood for food. Some eat the organic matter. Some eat the creatures grazing there. Look out for a wide variety of insects, especially beetles.

Look under logs and branches, pick up stones carefully and slowly. Hunt for rotten wood and leaf litter – lift it carefully with a twig. Remember to put logs and stones back in their original positions, and put the little creatures back in their homes.

Dead wood for lively minds

In any woodland, you can find good examples of dead wood in different states of decay. You can show children how dead wood can be quite light and crumbly. Bend a thin branch of living wood; see the difference when you bend a dead branch.

Let's go on a mini beast hunt

You need no expertise to find and observe minibeasts, and no equipment (though the list on page 108 can be useful). Most successful minibeast hunts are usually done in spring, summer and early autumn. Look under logs, look under stones; in the

UK there are no minibeasts that will hurt you, so there's no need to be afraid!

Keep your eyes open for a variety of spiders, ants, earwigs, millipedes, centipedes, woodlice and pill bugs (like woodlice, but they can roll up into a ball). Don't worry about knowing exactly what the creatures are. Chat over what they look like, what they are doing, and the way they move. You can always take a photo and later use a reference book or search online to identify them.

Put them back and treat them carefully. Use a piece of paper and let them crawl on it so you can look at them closely. You can let them crawl on you too if you're brave.

Is it OK to take some creatures home? It's not great for a creature to be taken from its environment. Some insects are protected by law and it is an offence to disturb them. There's a nice saying: take nothing but photos, leave nothing but footprints.

Homes in holes ... who lives here?

Rabbit holes – these are smaller than a dinner plate, usually more like a side plate; look for rabbit droppings around the entrance.

Smaller holes – if you see a golf ball-size hole, it could belong to a mouse, weasel, vole or stoat; near a riverbank and a little larger, it could be a water vole.

Fox holes – these are dinner plate-size holes, and very smelly!

Badger holes – these are larger than a dinner plate. An active set usually has a mound of earth outside, where they have cleared out the earth. Clear paths are usually visible around: they use the same paths under hedgerows. Look for places where they go through fences. Badgers do a deep clean each year and you can see their old bedding chucked out in spring time. Children like to know that badgers have their own special toilet, usually a little hole near the sett.

Millipedes and centipedes – which are which?

'Millipede' means a thousand legs, 'centipede' means a hundred legs, but they don't have that many: before you start counting, just look at one segment of the body. If you see clearly enough, you can spot two pairs of legs per segment on a millipede. Centipedes have one pair of legs per segment.

The real giveaway is the way they move. Centipedes are quick-moving predators. Millipedes are slow-moving plant eaters.

Who's been having dinner here?

Look out for evidence: nuts that are broken in half probably means squirrels; if they have been nibbled at, it's probably a mouse or a vole. If you find some pinecones very much eaten away down to the core, it's probably a squirrel, and look out for his dinner table too: squirrels like to put food on to a surface such as an old log.

Poo!

Children find animal poo funny and interesting. There's the 'ugh, disgusting' factor, and the inquisitive side. You can encourage both. For example, get them to come with you to a fox hole – seriously smelly. Or spot hedgehog poo, which looks like a black slug and smells like something else. Search for owl pellets maybe at the foot of an old tree: tread quietly as the owl may be snoozing above. Whose are these little droppings on little paths – sheep, deer or rabbits ... can we see any?

Snuffle, crunch! Hedgehogs

If you're lucky, you may come across a hedgehog in woodland, or a park or garden. You may hear it first: they often make very loud snuffly noises and crunch around in leaves. They are normally nocturnal, and avoid open spaces. They eat worms, slugs and snails, frogs, toads and lizards, berries, grass, leaves and fruit.

While most wild creatures move away fast when they sense danger, hedgehogs often freeze and start to roll into a ball, so you may have a good chance to observe one carefully. They have poor eyesight, good hearing and a very good sense of smell: try to approach without the wind behind you. Sit a few feet away, downwind, be VERY quiet and stay VERY still. After a few minutes you'll be rewarded with a little pointy black nose poking out and waving around. In a while it may straighten out and waddle off to a shady safe place.

In the garden with Grandad

Teenagers and adults often have lovely memories of gardening with their grandads. It's a great chance to get grubby together. And maybe eat things later.

Growing strawberries

For children, the greatest joys of gardening are closely linked with the pleasure of picking and eating fruit! What can be better than strawberries?

You will need

- hose or watering can
- two 25cm/10in terracotta or plastic pots, with holes in the base
- crocks – broken crockery or terracotta – or small bits of polystyrene
- multipurpose compost
- slow-release fertiliser

1 Water the strawberry plants about half an hour before repotting them.
2 Cover the bottom of the pots with crocks.
3 Half-fill the pots with compost. Sit the strawberries, still in their plastic container, in the compost: check that they'll be at least 2.5cm/1in below the rim of the pot when planted.
4 Carefully remove the plants from their containers and space them evenly around the pots. Add some slow-release fertiliser and fill in with compost around the plants. Press it between the plants with your fingers. Water well.
5 Show grandchildren how the plants are doing: how the flowers develop into small then larger berries, ripening from yellow (don't pick yet) to wonderful red. If you want a better crop next year, and fewer fruits but enough to keep young gardeners happy this year, remove half of the flowers as they appear.

A wonderful little water world

This could be a lovely treat for your grandchild, whether you have space in a garden or on a balcony – their own wild aquarium.

Given time, it will build up its own ecosystem. You never know what visitors will come ... waterskaters, dragonfly larvae, water mites, water snails. You can introduce a few by borrowing from friends' ponds.

You will need

- pond liner (available from a garden centre and aquatic specialist) or thick plastic sheeting
- hose or watering can
- hammer
- wide-headed galvanised nails or staples
- sharp knife or scissors
- aquatic plants, including a couple of oxygenating plants
- fine-meshed pond baskets
- pond gravel
- bricks or stones

1 Place the barrel where you want the mini-pond – it'll be hard to move when it's full. Push the pond liner into the pot, smoothing it over the bottom. There should be a good extra 15cm/6in of liner jutting above the top all round.

2 Pour in water to make the container about half full. This will push the liner down. Fold the liner over the edge and round the sides outside the barrel, leaving a good overlap.

3 Nail or staple the liner round the sides, then trim away the excess.

4 Prepare your aquatic plants in fine-meshed pond baskets, adding a layer of aquatic compost. Remove the plants from their containers, place them in the basket, fill around with more soil, then add a layer of pond gravel on top.

5 Put some bricks or large stones in the water, then place the baskets on top so that the gravel is just below the surface.

6 You need one or two oxygenating plants to keep your pond healthy. Plant them in pots, at the bottom.

7 After your pond has settled down for a few weeks, see if you can introduce some new guests. Take a glass jar full of water from a nearby pond – there may be interesting tiny creatures to look at in a magnifying glass, and microscopic eggs and larvae, which may thrive and grow in a new world. Borrow someone's water snails, frogspawn and even baby fish.

Interactive plants

Most plants don't provide much physical interaction. These three are interesting exceptions.

CAUGHT YOU! INSECTIVOROUS PLANTS

The idea of a plant luring and eating insects delights children. You can buy ones such as pitcher plants, sundews and bladderworts from some garden centres and specialist suppliers, and they'll be a great point of interest.

TICKLE IT UNDER THERE!

Sensitive plant – *Mimosa pudica* – is available from some garden centres. This little plant is fun to play with as it reacts to touch. Stroke it gently and the leaves all immediately fold in together.

POPPING FUCHSIAS!

Look out for fuchsia bushes that have many flowers. When the drop-like flowers reach maturity, they're ready for popping! Simply squeeze gently, and they pop open. You need to show children what flowers look ripe. In their enthusiasm they will probably squeeze some unripe ones, but it's no big deal – it doesn't normally harm the plant.

Sucking 'sturtiums!

Plant nasturtium seeds in a pot or garden, and they should come up every year in the spring and summer. As well as being very pretty, they're pretty tasty, too. The leaves and flowers add a peppery flavour to salads.

Kids love this: take a nasturtium flower, pinch a tiny piece of the end of the horn-like end, then suck from there and you'll get a lovely taste of nectar. The same trick also works for honeysuckle if you suck the end of the stamen that is attached to the middle of the flower.

Make a bee hotel

Solitary bees don't live in hives, but look for other interesting places to stay. You can provide one by creating a classy place at your home. Children can act as hotel inspectors to check occupancy from time to time.

You will need

- offcuts of planks of untreated wood about 15cm/6in long and 1.5cm/½in thick
- saw
- nails
- hammer
- reeds/hollow plant stems
- knife
- chunks of logs/blocks of untreated wood
- drill
- drill bit
- pencil
- pine cones

1 Make the box. This bee hotel starts as a simple box of nailed-together pieces of wood, with two compartments – as shown in the photo. Change the shape and size as you like, but give the roof a good overhang to keep off the rain.

2 Make the nesting tubes. Collect dead stems of hollow plants, reeds and bamboo. Cut them to about 15cm/6in lengths. Also collect old logs or blocks of untreated wood, then drill holes of varying sizes (between 3mm/⅛in and 5mm/¼in diameter) in them, 10–15cm/4–6in deep.

3 Fill the compartments. You can add pine cones for other visitors. Spiders will love you for that. Push everything tightly together.

4 Fix your box firmly (bees don't want a wobbly home) somewhere like a fence, a wall or a tree – about 1m/3ft 3in high, in a sunny position, facing south, near flowers and shrubs.

5 Wait and watch. On sunny days in spring and summer, adult female solitary bees may spot your lovely location. You may see them flying in carrying pollen, and little bits of debris to make cells along the tubes. If a tube is in use, a plug of mud or leaves means 'occupied, do not disturb'. The female lays eggs and leaves a food supply – pollen and nectar. The larvae will hatch the next year. You'll know they've flown the nest when the plug is opened.

"I help him hammer and saw things. He says I'm his special assistant."

Chapter 4

Making toys with a wow factor

Making things together is a very precious activity, and one that will stick in your grandchildren's memories probably for the rest of their lives.

This section has projects to delight children, to make with them, and for them. You'll see their eyes light up while you work. Find them jobs to do, and you'll increase their dexterity. Take time, and increase their concentration. Show them how to follow the instructions (that'll help their reading and comprehension) and also let their imaginations roam wider, to try different methods or patterns, or make up new projects.

Kitchen clatter

From the age of about eight months to two years, babies particularly love things that make a noise. They have very sensitive hearing, and notice very subtle differences in sounds, much more so than an adult. Rattles are sheer joy!

As well as any 'proper' rattles, it takes just minutes to create a set of different-sounding ones. Use small plastic bottles filled with a few assorted dried beans or other good noise makers, such as screws and nuts and bolts. With different sounds and different weights, these provide great interest. Just be sure your grandchild hasn't yet learned how to undo bottle caps!

Some of the best toys are free and in your kitchen. Once a baby can sit up, pans and lids, wooden spoons, mixing bowls and pots to put things in all make lovely noises. Bunches of keys are usually a wow anywhere.

A pretty mobile to move with the times

This will entrance a tiny baby, and then small children. It can be a great project to do with an older brother or sister for a new arrival.

Change the components as they grow older. Once they've learned to focus, small babies love following movement. At first they see dark and light shapes most clearly, so start with simple black and white shapes on the mobile. By around the age of three months, they will enjoy colour. From 18 months, add some family photos: they'll like you, mum and dad to talk about at bedtime.

Fixing: make sure the mobile is well out of reach of a baby. Hang it from a hook on the ceiling. Alternatively, two pieces of dowel and duct tape on the bars of a cot can do the trick.

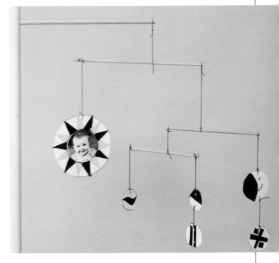

You will need
- 3 lengths of 3–6mm/⅛–¼in dowel:
  1 piece 30cm/12in;
  1 piece 24cm/10in;
  1 piece 21cm/8in
- craft/utility knife
- fine-grade abrasive paper
- ruler
- pencil
- thin card/stock or thick cardboard
- black, white and coloured paper
- scissors
- glue and/or paint and paintbrush
- hole punch, or something spikey to make holes through cardboard
- thread

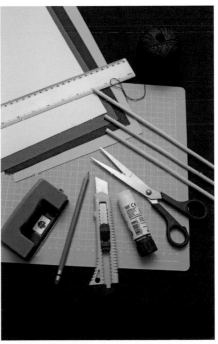

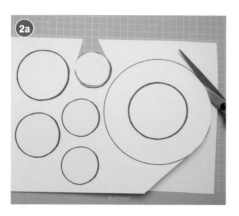

1. Cut and smooth the lengths of dowel.
2. Cut the six shapes in card, as in the photo. Here the circles are 5cm/2in, 8cm/3in and 15cm/6in diameter. Decorate them with coloured paper or paint. Aim for an interesting contrast between the two sides of any shape.
3. Punch a hole at the top of each shape, two holes at the top and bottom of the smaller pieces.
4. Tie the moon, sun and smaller pieces to three pieces of thread. Make a little noose or slip knot at the ends.
5. Balancing can be fiddly. The trick is to work from the bottom up. Get the bottom arm balanced first, then the next up, then the top. Tie a component (or two) to each end of the dowel. Find the balancing point on your finger, moving the components along the dowel if necessary. To help things balance, you can trim a little card off one of the components to reduce weight, or wind some thread at one end of dowel to add weight.
6. Hang your mobile up. It's ready to float around!

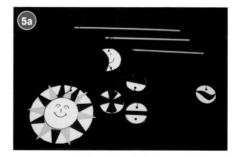

Dreamcatcher

Here's a lovely thing to make with treasures picked up on the beach or in the woods. It can hang by a window, turning gently and catching dreams and memories like a spider catches flies!

You will need

- 3 thin branches or 5mm–10mm/¼–½in dowel rod
- string and/or coloured yarn
- craft/utility knife
- feathers, leaves, coloured fabric, any other treasures you've collected (see below)

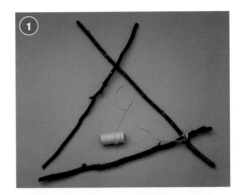

1 Make a triangle with the wood, binding the pieces together with string.
2 Tie a long piece of thread at one corner. Carry it along one side, up and over at roughly 7.5cm/3in intervals, all the way round, and fix with a knot.
3 With more thread, tie to one loop, and criss-cross the triangle to create a kind of spider's web, each time wrapping the thread once around a loop. Tie the thread to secure it when you're pleased with the result.

4 Now add some things to the web. Do you have any feathers? Any little pieces of coloured fabric? You can add small photos, dried grasses, secret messages, a lock of hair, little drawings – wherever your dreams take you. Tie some threads to hang at the bottom and add things there.
5 Finally, tie thread at the top ready for hanging your dreamcatcher at the window.

Stilts

'Look at me, Grandad, aren't I tall!'

Children love playing on stilts. With a little help, and encouragement from seeing you falling off, it doesn't take long for them to get the knack.

If you're making these for a young child you may need to reduce the wood sizes. The tops of the stilts need to be shaped into handles, here rather big for small hands. Choose your wood carefully, as

knot-free as possible for the uprights, otherwise a knot will almost certainly turn up just where you don't want it!

These stilts have adjustable footrests fitted by coach bolts, with holes bored at intervals. To adjust the footrest, remove the coach bolts, move it up or down and replace the bolts.

You will need
- timber:
  - legs – 2 pieces 44 x 38mm/nominal 2 x 1½in planed timber, 1.8cm/6ft long
  - footrests – 4 pieces 12mm/nominal ½in plywood, 15 x 10cm/6 x 4in
  - footrest cores – 2 pieces 44 x 38mm/nominal 2 x 1½in planed timber, 10.8cm/4in long
- tape measure
- pencil
- saw
- clamps/cramps or masking tape
- cutting block
- carpenter's square
- wood glue
- bradawl or awl
- screws
- screwdriver
- tenon saw
- fine-grade abrasive paper
- power drill
- drill bits
- countersink bit
- 4 M10 x 75mm/3in coach bolts with nuts or wing nuts
- adjustable spanner
- chisel
- stanley knife
- smoothing plane
- wood paint and paintbrush (optional)

1 The uprights are longer than necessary to allow for two offcuts that will form part of the footrest. Clamp or tape both uprights together. Mark the length of the legs, and then the two short footrest stubs. Saw the legs to length.

2 Cut the footrest stubs to length, then put them to one side. Note the use of a cutting block in this photo.

3 With the leg uprights taped or clamped together, mark the positions for the footrests, ensuring that the spacing intervals are equal. Mark across both legs using a carpenter's square. Don't drill the coach bolt holes yet.

4 Each footrest is a wooden 'sandwich' – two pieces of plywood with a timber filling. Squirt plenty of wood glue on both sides of the filling. Put the sandwich together and drive in screws from both sides. Beware· timber sandwiched like this has a tendency to slide, so watch out that pieces don't slip out of place while you're screwing the blocks together.

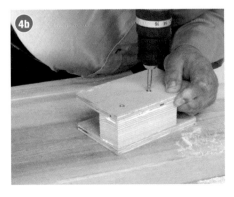

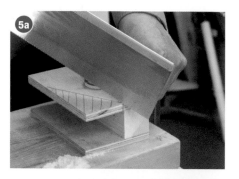

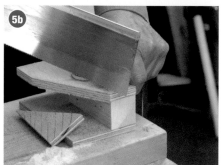

5 Clamp the footrest to the bench. Using a tenon saw, cut off the corner (following the hatched area on the photograph). Repeat on the other side.

6 Sand down the footrest to remove all the sharp corners. Children's ankles and legs will be in contact with the footrests, so make them nice and smooth.

7 Take one footrest and align its top edge with one of the spaced lines that you drew in Step 3. Fit a cramp to hold the footrest to the leg and mark the two holes that need to be drilled. Drill holes in the footrest and leg for the bolt bolts.

8 Having drilled the first pair of holes, move the footrest along to align with the next pencil line, and mark and drill the next pair of holes. Repeat the process until you have as many holes as you need.

9 Fix the footrests in place using coach bolts. The square shank at the top, just below the rounded head, will grip the timber when the bolt is fastened on the other side. Tighten the nuts using a spanner.

10 With both footrests fitted, the stilts are complete. To prevent the bottoms of the legs from becoming ragged, use a plane or knife to chamfer all four edges. Make sure that the tops of the legs are nicely rounded off.

11 If you intend to paint the stilts, leave the areas where the footrests go paint-free (paint makes the legs thicker: the footrests will spoil the paintwork when they're adjusted up and down).

Bow and arrows

Playing with bows and arrows is great fun. This bow is simple to make. It should be about to about the height of the child's eyes, so adjust these measurements accordingly.

You will need

- 30mm x 5mm/nominal 1 x ¼in strip wood, 2 pieces 1m/3ft 3in, 2 pieces 30cm/12in
- saw
- tape measure
- pencil
- drill
- drill bits
- wood glue
- glue spreader
- screws
- screwdriver
- clamp
- about 3.8m/12½ft string
- craft/utility knife
- fine-grade abrasive paper
- material for the grip – duct tape, cloth, towelling grip, tennis handle binding
- thin dowel or bamboo
- file (optional)
- pen cap, screwdriver bit or drill bit
- duct tape
- goose, turkey or swan feathers or thin card/stock or foam plastic

For the bow

1 Drill a small hole through all four pieces of wood centrally at their midpoint, i.e. 15cm/6in and 50cm/20in.

2 Lay out the four pieces, then spread glue generously on one side of every piece.

3 Stick them together with the shorter pieces on the outside and the longer in the middle. Using a small screw in the drill hole made at Step 1, screw the pieces together. Line them up, then clamp them.

4 Drill a hole about 5mm/¼in wide about 2cm/¾in in from either end.

5 Thread about 2.5m/8ft 2in of the string through, around and back along the full length of the bow, so you can pull it tight to get the wood to curve. Do not force the wood. Knot in position.

6 Use clamps or knots to hold the strips tightly together. Leave the glue to dry.

7 Remove the string and clamps. Trim the wood with a craft knife and sand them to take any corners off the handle area.

8 Wrap binding around the middle to make a handle, fixing it with glue or tape.

9 Cut a new piece of string about 1.3m/4ft 4in and thread it through the holes. Tie a knot at one end, tighten the string, then tie a knot at the other end.

For the arrow

10 Use a thin dowel or bamboo. To fly well, an arrow needs (a) to be straight, (b) to have some weight at the front, (c) to have flights at the back, and (d) to have a notch for the string. Make the notch with a craft knife or file.

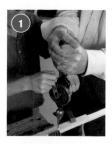

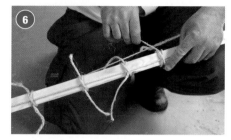

11 For the arrowheads, try taping on a pen cap, a screwdriver bit or a drill bit. Wrap with duct tape for safety.

12 Good feathers for flights are difficult to find, unless you know where there are some geese, turkeys or swans. Other feathers are too weak to be much use, but look pretty so may please a child. Fortunately, you can use various other materials, such as thin card or foam plastic, fixed with glue or duct tape.

13 The flights should be applied in threes, positioned at equal distances round the shaft. One flight should be at right angles to the notch.

Balsa glider

This model is simple enough for many children aged 11+ to learn to make, if they're reasonably accurate at measuring and marking and safe with a very sharp knife.

You need just one standard craft sheet of balsa, which will leave you with leftovers for spare parts; 2mm/¹⁄₁₆in thickness is easy to cut. The downside is that your glider will be on the heavy side. Once your grandchild has gained confidence, experiment with thinner balsa for longer flights.

You will need

- 1 standard sheet of 2mm/¹⁄₁₆in balsa wood, 75 x 790mm/3 x 30in or two 75 x 450mm/3 x 18in
- ruler
- pencil
- straight edge for cutting
- very sharp craft/utility knife or scalpel
- marker pens
- balsa cement or strong PVA wood glue
- Blu Tack or non-hardening modelling clay

1 Mark and cut the balsa sheet as shown in the diagram. Draw guidelines as shown on the fuselage and wing.

2 Now's the time to decorate the fuselage, wing and tail pieces with marker pens, making it look really cool.

3 Glue the tail pieces on to the fuselage, as accurately as possible, at right angles. Glue the tail fin, in line with the fuselage, also as accurately as possible.

4 Glue the wing under the fuselage, as squarely as possible.

5 Fix some Blu Tack firmly on to the nose. Find the glider's centre of balance by lightly holding it under the fuselage between forefinger and thumb. It should balance on your finger at around the midpoint, under the wing. Add a blob of Blu Tack or non-hardening modelling clay to improve the balance if necessary. Now you're ready to fly!

15mm = ½in
20mm = ¾in
70mm = 2¾in
75mm = 3in
300mm = 12in
360mm = 14in

70

75   20
      20

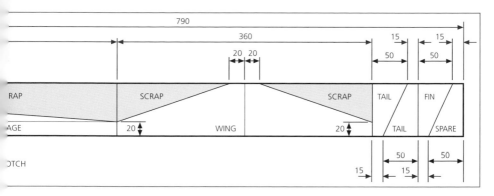

						790		
RAP	SCRAP		20 20	SCRAP	TAIL	FIN	
AGE		20	WING	20	TAIL	SPARE	
OTCH							

3

LAUNCH TIPS

A long, gentle, level throw is more effective than a sudden launch (children tend to chuck gliders upwards). You may have to adjust the blob of sticky stuff for different types of flight. Also, you may find your glider will fly well upside down as well as the right way up!

Launching with an elastic band works well at a slight angle, up to 20–30 degrees. Children love shooting at higher angles – the results can be spectacular, but things can also get out of control.

This plane can sometimes travel a long way, so only fly it in a large garden or open space. And have some spare ready-cut pieces to hand, plus glue and a craft/utility knife to be ready for instant repairs.

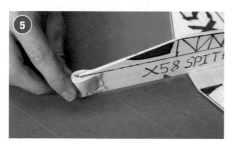

4

5

Weapons and wands!

Fabulous fairy wand

You can make some great magic wands in no time at all – hey presto!
This one works well in the dark.

You will need

- 2 sheets of A4/Letter size paper
- 1cm/½in dowel rod, about 30cm/12in long, or a long-handled wooden spoon
- small pencil torch (optional)
- adhesive tape
- pencil
- gold or silver thin card/stock
- craft/utility knife
- strips and pieces of coloured and/or glittery materials
- PVA glue, spreader and glue pot (optional)

1 Roll the paper around the dowel or wooden spoon to get it ready to make the paper form a long tube, to fit over the torch.

2 Tape the paper tube along its edge, then tape it to the torch. Alternatively, just roll the paper and tape it along its edge, without the torch.

3 Draw and cut out a star in thin card, and tape it to one end of the paper tube.

4 Tape or glue strips of fabric or paper to the star and wind a ribbon round the handle to finish.

Lumos – a wicked wizard's wand

This is made in a very similar way as the fairy wand.

You will need

- brown/Kraft wrapping paper or an old or new manila envelope
- 1cm/½in dowel rod, about 30cm/12in long, or a long-handled wooden spoon
- A4/Letter size envelope
- adhesive tape
- small pencil torch
- piece of white paper, about 2 x 10cm/¾ x 4in
- craft/utility knife

1 Cut the brown paper to about 30 x 20cm/12 x 8in.

2 Roll the paper around the dowel or wooden spoon to get it ready to make the paper form a long tube, to fit over the torch.

3 Tape the paper tube along its edge, then tape it to the torch.

4 Roll the piece of white paper and fit it into the top of the wand, peeping out by about 1cm/½in. Glue it or tape it.

5 It's almost ready. Just say 'Lumos' and switch the torch on … hey presto!

Super light sabre

Fans of the *Star Wars* movies will feel the force with one of these.

You will need

- adhesive tape
- red or blue coloured cellophane (optional)
- small torch
- 3 3mm/¼in dowel rods, about 30cm/12in long, or long skewers
- A3 sheet of aper
- narrow rolling pin, or 3cm/1¼in dowel rod
- duct tape
- translucent plastic bottle lid, about 2.5cm/1in diameter

1 Tape the coloured cellophane, if you have any, to the torch lens.
2 Tape the dowel rods around the torch to make a supporting frame for the paper.
3 Roll the paper around the rolling pin to get it curling.

4 Fix it around the torch with duct tape and tape all the way up its length with adhesive tape.
5 Fix the bottle lid to the top of the paper. . Switch on the torch and you're ready for intergalactic battles.

Swashbuckling pirate's cutlass

You will need

- corrugated cardboard
- ruler
- pencil
- craft/utility knife or scissors
- PVA glue or adhesive tape
- gold and silver marker pens
  or paint

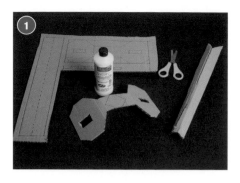

1 Mark out and cut the pieces of cardboard following the photo. Make sure the corrugation lines run lengthways on the blade and crossways on the hand guard. The length of the blade depends on the size of the child.

2 Draw a line firmly along the middle of the blade with a pencil.

3 Use the ruler to fold it in half lengthways; cut to a point to finish the blade.

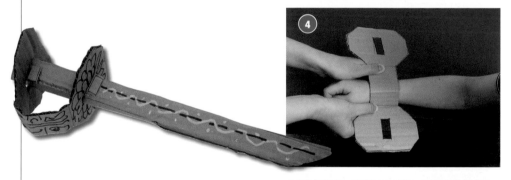

4 Bend the thin part of the hand guard over your grandchild's wrist.

5 Slip each end over the top of the blade.

6 Hold the hand guard in position. Glue the eight small rectangles on to the blade. You need to stick them on all sides (see the large photo on page 137.)

7 Leave to dry, then decorate if you like. Now it's time for battle…

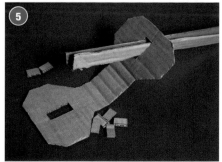

Corrugated cardboard creations

Flatpack furniture, household appliances … things that arrive in large cardboard boxes can be the starting point of all sorts of models and temporary toys. And if you're a customer at a local greengrocer, the chances are that they'll happily supply you with old banana boxes (supermarkets may be less obliging).

Once you've got a big box, it can provide great opportunities for imaginative play, such as becoming:

- for a one-year-old – a box for putting things in and taking them out
- for a two-year-old – a hiding place
- for a three-year-old – a boat to sail in
- for a four-year-old – a dolly's bed

- for a five-year-old – a spaceman's helmet

Corrugated castle

This makes a great place for play, and is easily assembled and disassembled. You can use the same method for making other large corrugated play buildings. This particular design uses standard pallet-size sheets. It's worth buying extras for repairs, mistakes and other constructions. Use the templates to mark up the sheets, then cut out the shapes. Slots need to be about 5mm/¼in wide, very slightly more than the thickness of the cardboard. Follow the direction of corrugations on the photos to ensure maximum strength.

You will need

- 6 sheets of double-wall corrugated cardboard, standard pallet size 1 x 1.2m/3ft 3in x 4ft30cm/12in and 1m/3ft 3in rulers (or use a piece of timber)
- carpenter's square
- tape measure
- marker pen or soft pencil
- very sharp strong craft/utility knife with spare blades
- cutting board or scrap plywood sheet to protect surfaces
- glue – woodworking PVA or hot melt

1 Mark and cut out all the small pieces:

Sheet 1
- 10 strengthening bars (shape A) 9 x 102cm/3½ x 40in

Sheet 2
- 2 more strengthening bars (shape A)
- 4 corner brackets (shape B) – 20 x 9cm/8 x 3½in
- 8 bars for the rectangular windows (shape C) – about 3 x 35cm/1¼ x 14in
- 3 templates:
  shape D for cross shaped windows – 9cm/3 ½in x27cm/10 ½in squares
  shape E for rectangular windows – 25cm/10in x 35cm/14in
  shape F - 7cm/3in x 15cm/6in for the tops of the walls (crenellations);
- shape G for the doors - 25cm/10in x 50cm/20in

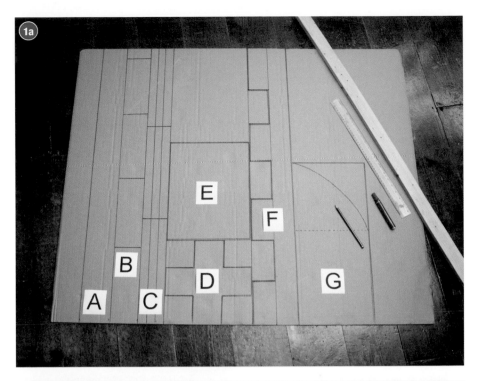

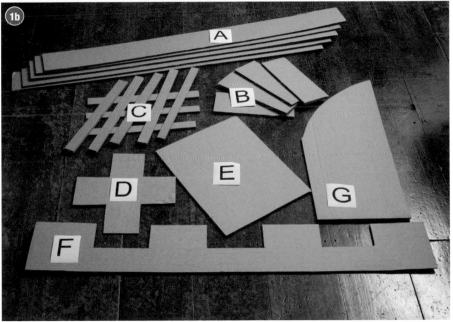

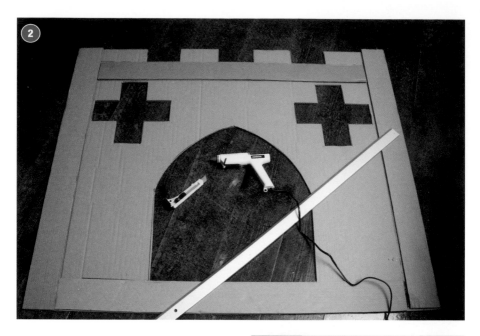

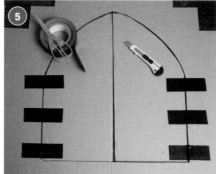

2 Mark up and cut the walls

Sheets 3 and 4
- back and front, with doors and windows

Sheets 5 and 6
- two side walls, with windows

3 Use the templates to mark up the sheets: cut out the shapes.

4 Slots need to be about 5mm/¼in wide, very slightly more than the thickness of your cardboard.

5 Mark and cut out the front and back doors. Trim about 5mm/¼in all around to help them fit back in. Tape them back onto the panels with duct tape inside and out hinges.

6 Glue all the strengthening bars (shape

A) on each panel, top and bottom and either side inside each wall.

7 Fix the bars to the rectangular windows with duct tape on the inside.

8 Time to assemble your castle. The front and back pieces slot onto the side walls. Each corner piece slots in at the top corners of two walls. To disassemble: simply lift the front and back off, you'll now have a nice flat pack castle, ready for any visiting young princesses or knights!

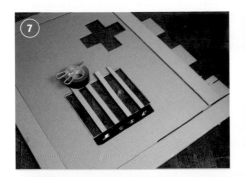

The author

Andrew Parkinson's somewhat haphazard career has involved him in a series of things beginning with M: museums, music management, marketing and most recently Manuals for Haynes. He contributed large chunks to the *Dad Manual*, and wrote the *Spy* and *Pirate Manuals* for children. He has been a copywriter for over 30 years, writing on all kinds of subjects, from bouncing babies to jumbo jets, from art to zoos. He lives in Devon, close by one of the oldest public play parks in Britain, where his four grandchildren and many of the other children in this book often play.

Acknowledgements

Many thanks to the many mums and dads, young and old, and ever youthful grandads and grandmas who have shared great ideas and experience, and checked out and (usually) given the thumbs up to the activities in this book. Particular thanks to Dick Brown, James Bushell, Jo and Andy Frost, Jo and Chris Frost, Emma Funnell, John Hart, Mark Macnair, Lester Williams and Alan Wooderson.

And many thanks to all the children who played themselves for the camera, in particular Lily Allan; Isabelle and Jack Anderson; Carys Blacklock; Harry Clarke; Amy, Aiden and Alice Cole; Carlie and Callum Culverhouse; Amelia Dobson; Ella and Dylan Emmet; Isaac and Reuben Evans; George and Alice Farrell; Etty and Henry Funnell; Poppy and Olly Frost; Eloise and Talitha Frost; Ruari and Rupert Frost; Tom Gale; Ernest and Seren Horsley-Whyman; Hazel Haworth; Jake and Aaron Joiner; Ava and Elise Kimble; Jasper and Darcy Lonsdale-McCreadie; Jacob, Sam and Thomas Moffatt; Emily and Harriet Newton; Megan and Rory Pimperton; William and Isabelle Potter; Alvie Russell; Ellie and Jacob Rowles; Chloe, Reuben and Levi Sambrooks; Coco Stirrat; Sophia, Joanna and Beatrice White.

I am very grateful to Diana Dean and What About the Children – a charity that promotes the emotional needs of the under-threes (www.whataboutthechildren.org.uk) – for feeding me with some very valuable and interesting information.

And special thanks to my wife Jacqui for providing me with a perfect set of grandchildren to learn from and play with.